ELEMENTARY TEACHER'S GUIDE TO WORKING WITH PARENTS

ELEMENTARY TEACHER'S GUIDE TO WORKING WITH PARENTS

Helen Heffernan and Vivian Edmiston Todd

formerly Chief,
Bureau of Elementary
Education, California
State Department of
Education

Curriculum Specialist

PARKER PUBLISHING COMPANY, INC., WEST NYACK, N.Y.

A WORD TO THE TEACHER

As soon as methods of teaching and classroom management are under control, the teacher turns attention to working with the adults who exert the greatest influence on the lives of children—their parents. Mothers and fathers are with their children the greater part of each twenty-four hours, and they are legally responsible for them. When teachers and administrators work with parents for the good of the children, much can be accomplished. But when a parent works at odds with the school, or fails to reinforce what the school is trying to do, he can negate much that the school endeavors to teach and can harass school personnel because children reflect critical parental attitudes in their school relations. Teachers and administrators who realize the importance of parental attitudes in the educative process, constantly attempt to improve their ways of working with parents.

Underlying the various techniques that make for good rapport between school and parents are three all pervasive rules of action:

- Provide a setting and supporting framework that furthers mutual confidence at all times.
- Believe that parents are doing the best that they can in terms of:
    - what they know
    - the resources they have at their command
    - the values and beliefs of their social group.
- Be objective and realistic and, at the same time, courteous and considerate.

The school works with parents not only as the persons closest to its pupils but also as a community nucleus through which to build a climate favorable to school success. Parents are the members of the community most apt to endorse school bond issues and other measures to further the work of the school with children. Parental enthusiasm for the school is a major asset. Parents who understand school policies and procedures,

9

curricular objectives and programs, are prepared to encourage neighborly support for the school as well as to motivate their children in facing school tasks with energy and effort.

A teacher or a school administrator can usually count on and make use of parental backing for school policies and practices so long as he is working with middle-class families. But when he works in a community setting different from his style of life, a school person needs to enlarge his repertoire of methods of working with parents.

The basic plan presented in this book about working with parents—all kinds of parents, is as follows:

- Know yourself as a member of the middle class steeped in its ideas and values, hemmed in by its restraints, and upheld by its virtues.
- Capitalize on the attitudes and practices that you have in common with middle-class families when you work with them.
- Help the children and their families from social groups other than middle class to solve their problems in keeping with their particular socioeconomic situation. In teaching children the basic skills at the point where they are in their learning, avoid expecting too much from them and their parents.
- Explain your personal or middle-class point of view when it is at variance with the point of view of parents, but be tolerant about its not being adopted immediately or applied outside of school.
- Select and use techniques appropriate to the situation and especially those furthering the development of each child.

ACKNOWLEDGMENTS

Elementary Teacher's Guide to Working with Parents was written out of professional backgrounds combined with parental experience and interaction with parents. To enumerate the many writers, co-workers, and friends who have contributed to the book is not possible. But it is possible to recognize the cooperation of the Long Beach (California) Unified School District and especially the willingness of principals, counselors, and teachers to discuss their pleasure and problems in working with parents, and to make segments of their experience available to others. Such professional contributions to this book are gratefully acknowledged.

CONTENTS

ELEMENTARY
TEACHER'S GUIDE
TO WORKING WITH PARENTS

Chapter One

DEVELOPING
THE BASIS
FOR A
CONFERENCE_____

Working with parents is not only a desirable, but also an essential, part of working with children. A school person can increase his effectiveness with children immeasurably if he reinforces his work with a child by interaction with the child's parents. A child is influenced greatly by his teacher, but he is influenced most by his parents. This influence is understandable in terms of the confidence that he has in a parent who has gone with him through emotional experience after emotional experience, who has cared for him more than anyone else has, and who continues to extend close relationship through the associations of out-of-school hours. To capitalize on parental influence as an aid to teaching a child is imperative. The wise school person constantly enlarges his ability to work with parents effectively, both individually and in general groups, in conference, in committee, and in community gathering.

Mutual Confidence

Mutual confidence is the framework within which effective school and home relationships occur. The school respects the responsibility of the parent, and values what he is able to do with his children within the limitations that he has. Such respect on the part of the school for the parents is mirrored by parental respect for the school.

How is this mutual confidence built?

When Susie's teacher sees Susie on the street or in the market place, she takes time to say, "Hello," and to introduce herself to whomever Susie is shopping with. "How do you do? I am Mrs. Jones, and Susie is one of my girls in the fifth grade at the Carver School."

If the parent, relative, or neighbor who is with Susie does not respond by introducing herself, Mrs. Jones may continue the conversation with some neutral topic such as the weather or the daily news, hoping to pick up some cues to identity as she conveys her appreciation of Susie as a fine person. Or, Mrs. Jones may simply inquire, "What is your name?" and follow her inquiry with a sincere statement: "I am glad to meet you."

No matter what the precise conversation, Mrs. Jones endeavors to convey both to Susie and her companion her genuine interest in Susie and in her family and associates.

Mutual confidence between the school and the parents is also built up in the conversations among teachers and other school personnel. The teacher who refers to a pupil as "a brat," or to a parent in a belittling tone of voice, is apt to carry over such ego-reducers into actual conversations with children and parents, to the detriment of good relationships with them. But the teacher who is sincerely interested in each child and the people who are important in the life of the child, talks of them and to them sincerely and appreciatively.

The principal's office, as well as the shopping center and the teachers' room, is a place for building mutual confidence between parents and school. A parent who has ventured into a school and is a little unsure about talking with someone there can either feel repulsed, ignored, or welcomed. The wise principal sees to it that the office is a place which immediately welcomes anyone coming in. A warm welcome not only sets at ease the timid parent but also reassures the angry parent, who will cool his temper when he realizes that the school is not belligerent.

If the principal is not in the office, or is on his way to an appointment, he should be sure that the secretary will help the parent by arranging a convenient time to confer and by finding out what the problem seems to be. A secretary who takes a real interest in children and parents can create a favorable setting for the pending conference.

The office secretary should appreciate her role as an interpreter of the school to children and parents. If she interrupts her desk work to receive a visitor reassuringly, she has reduced the friction which could have interfered with school-parent relationships.

"How do you do? May I help you?" Or, "Good morning. Would you like to see Miss Duncan, the principal?" Such cordial greetings in response to the appearance of a visitor assures him that he is in a climate favorable to learning and to the accomplishment of constructive purposes.

To assist his secretary in receiving people pleasantly, the principal is careful to explain what he is doing in the same way that he wants her to explain his activities to others. "I shall be at a meeting of principals this morning. If you need to reach me, telephone 444-4444," he may say. This gives his secretary the cue that enables her to say to a visitor, "I am sorry that Mr. Friend is not here now. He is attending a principals' meeting this morning, but will be here this afternoon. Would you be able to come back at 2:00 o'clock?" If an emergency arises, she will use the telephone number he has given her. But almost all matters can be taken care of on an interim basis by following the simple rule: *Make each parent's contact with the school a pleasant and constructive one.*

Attention to Children

School personnel and parents work together for two purposes:

- To further the best interests of children.
- To assist an individual child in solving his problems of development.

Working together for the good of the school as a social institution is one aspect of furthering the best interests of children.

Attention to individual cases leads to improved plans for working with the group. When the school has considered with parents the detailed problems of their child, the school people are in a better position to help another child with such problems, and to help groups of children avoid similar problems. Attention to an individual child's problems is not completed until it has been evaluated and plans made for improved practices in the future.

Each child develops through coping with a sequence of problems. Usually he has adequate adult assistance with his problems through his parents and through the experiences that the school provides for his class. But when the problems are too great and their solution gets beyond the child's control, he needs help. If his parents are unable to help him, they may seek aid from the school. If his problems in the school situation are too great, the school should initiate parent conferences in an effort to provide the child with assistance that he needs. In either case, parents and school personnel should join forces to help the child. They can evaluate their joint efforts in terms of the improved ability of the child to cope with the problems that confront him.

Group Differences Among Parents

Teachers think of their pupils as individuals within the classroom group. They think of families as individuals within the social group of the community. Each family is unique and each parent is an interesting person to meet because of relationships between his behavior and that of the child whom the teacher works with daily. In some instances the shyness or the brashness of a parent suggests that he has not solved his own problems of human relationships, and this may be reflected in the behavior of his child. In other instances a parent may have the same alert look that his boy has, or the delightful sense of humor that his daughter often displays.

Getting to know parents as individuals and getting to know the individuality of a family are easy when a teacher has a frame of reference to help her in grouping them. For example, one such frame of reference is rate of learning. People learn at different speeds, depending upon their learning abilities and upon the experience they have had with what is to be learned. A teacher gears her teaching to the rate of learning of a child and his family. For instance, if she is giving her name to a parent whose accent shows experience with the sounds and tonal patterns of a language other than English, she is careful to spell out the name slowly and to repeat it distinctly.

The frame of reference that is especially useful to school personnel in working with parents is the classification of people into social classes.[1] W. Lloyd Warner and others used anthropological methods to describe the social structure of a New England community. An older American community, they thought, would have become more visibly and firmly structured than the new suburban communities with shifting populations of younger people. These anthropologists interviewed the members of

[1] Earl E. Edgar, *Social Foundations of Education.* New York: The Center for Applied Research in Education, Inc., 1965. Chapter III is concerned with "Social Stratification."

the adult community and found out the practices and opinions of each family by such questions as:

"Whom do you have dinner with?"
"Whom would you like to have invite you to dinner?"
"Whom would you like to avoid dining with?"

Putting together the interview material showed that the community had groups of families with each group characterized by behavior unique for that group. For instance, one group valued old chairs and dishes which had been used by previous generations and carefully handed down from generation to generation. Another group in the community valued new items of these kinds, and prided itself on buying the latest household furnishings that had come on the market.

The school person who has worked for years in the same community gradually comes to know its different groups of families. When he meets Family A for the first time and notes its friendship with Family B whom he already knows, he can guess about, and later verify, its attitudes about school and children. An experienced teacher usually can identify the extent to which a family is either interested in children and supportive of learning and educational institutions, disinterested in them, or openly antagonistic to them. Over the years he also becomes familiar with other attitudes of families that are characteristic of the social group with which they identify and probably are indirectly pertinent to the progress of their children in school—for instance, interest in taking responsibility.[2]

New Tools for the Teacher

Thanks to the social anthropologists studying and describing the social structure of communities in the United States, school personnel have new techniques and new tools with which to work. W. Lloyd Warner has devised a scale with which to identify the socioeconomic status of a family.[3] Research workers apply the interview technique of the anthropologist and raise significant questions, such as *Who Shall Be Educated?*[4]

With the help of the social anthropologist, the administrator, the

[2] Erving Goffman, *The Presentation of Self in Everyday Life.* New York: Doubleday and Company, 1959.

[3] W. Lloyd Warner, *Social Class in America.* New York: Harper Publishers, 1960.

[4] W. Lloyd Warner, Robert J. Havighurst, and M. B. Loeb, *Who Shall Be Educated?* New York: Harper and Brothers Publishers, 1944.

teacher, and other school personnel can use questions significant in determining social groupings in the community. These questions include:

- What schooling do families expect their children to have?
- What roles do the families expect to play in the community?
- Is the school a help or a hindrance to obtaining these goals?
- What skills do the families have for earning money?
- How much money do the families earn a year, and what does the family income buy for the family?

Through the help of the findings of research in human relations, school personnel can raise significant questions as they become acquainted with the child and his family. These questions include:

- Which members of his family feel that this child is an important person?
- Does the child have self-confidence?
- What opportunities does the school provide for him to have a feeling of importance?
- What opportunities does his school class provide for him to have a responsible role?

Social Classification of the School Person

To benefit from the work of the social anthropologist, the school person should come to know his own social classification, together with the points of view and the beliefs, attitudes and practices that are an integral part of his social group. Generally, social anthropologists speak of the teacher as a member of the middle class, and the school as a middle-class institution. Thus the school and the teacher are identified with the largest social class and with the manners and morals that characterize the nation as a whole.

The middle class upholds the national traditions. It values the cultural heritage and the schools which pass this on to coming generations. Its members appreciate the family and further family stability. They uphold the institution of marriage and regret the phenomenon of divorce. Christianity and moral principles are basic in the culture and in the middle class. So also are the courtship customs and the bathroom practices which are considered proper. Business is furthered by members of the middle class both as consumers and as responsible workers. The schools are a means to a good position and economic stability for the family.

The preparation of teachers and other school personnel is carried on within middle-class ideology. School people are alert to identify potential teachers. They are apt to select people like themselves— people of similar ways of living, with beliefs in what characterizes the middle class. When teachers are guided through general education into teaching, the process is a middle-class sifting. The professorial committee that selects those college students who are to take practice teaching and complete their requirements for a teaching credential is probably not aware of itself as a committee of middle-class people selecting those who will become leaders in the community in promoting middle-class standards. Nevertheless, its selection of prospective teachers is apt to be a simultaneous selection of subject-matter teachers and purveyors of middle-class manners and morals.

When the son or daughter of an immigrant family becomes a teacher, the family is assured of being an integral part of the social structure of its new country. He or she has demonstrated knowledge about how to select middle-class costumes appropriate for teachers, how to speak as middle-class people do without use of profanity or other improper speech patterns, and how to enjoy sport, civic, religious, cultural, and other activities enjoyed by middle-class people.

Social Distance Affects Conferring

When a school person and a parent have the same outlook on children, the same basic values, and the same ways of talking, they find it easy to discuss problems as they arise. They find it easy to arrange a time and place to confer about problems of the children. The middle-class parent is at home in an elementary school. He probably has an aunt, a cousin, or a friend who teaches, and some sympathy for the problems that they face. He has pleasant memories of his own days in elementary school. As it fits into his life, he participates in school-initiated activities. If the principal calls to suggest a conference, he comes willingly to the school. In fact, if he has already met the principal, he discusses the problem over the telephone when the principal calls, and may not need to come to the school for a further conference.

The woman teacher and the middle-class mother also find it easy to communicate. For Jane's teacher to call or write a note about Jane is much like having the Brownie or Bluebird leader call or write a note about the next meeting of Jane's group. A request to come to school is treated like any other invitation. Furthermore, attending a school event is much like attending an event at the church. It is an expected activity; a parent fits the activity into his life if he can do so conveniently.

But as soon as the easy communication within one social class is replaced by the necessity for communication across the social distance that exists between social classes, complications arise. The school person finds it difficult to climb the hill to the large house that symbolizes the domination of its owner over the affairs of the community. He also finds it difficult to cross the tracks to the poor little shack in shanty town. In both situations he wonders, "How will I be received? Will I be able to make the people understand?" He finds it easy to postpone going up the hill or across the tracks. Finally, when the problem has not been solved and the pressure for its solution has mounted, he crosses the social distance between himself and the parents. But the effort of doing so does not add to his ease in talking with them, nor to the probability of success in making his points.

The parents who live in the big house on the hill are used to receiving invitations to community events. An invitation to a school event is as easily put into the wastebasket as is any other invitation. In ignoring the school invitation, the parents are not being rude. They just are not accustomed to including such events in the pattern of their lives.

One elementary school teacher, Miss Frank, who had lived in a large house set back from the street amid gardens and terraces, had in her class Catherine, the daughter of a leading family. Miss Frank realized Catherine's loneliness. In her class, Catherine did not share the companionship of the walk home after school with the other children. Instead, she left school by herself to step into the car waiting to take her home. Her only opportunity to play games with her classmates was during the recess periods of the school day.

When Catherine's birthday was a few weeks away, Miss Frank telephoned Catherine's mother to ask if she might call Thursday afternoon after school. Catherine's mother was very glad to have Miss Frank come on Thursday, although as a general rule she did not receive callers that day of the week. She was most receptive to Miss Frank's suggestion that Catherine gain experience in being a hostess by having classmates at a birthday party. Miss Frank made specific suggestions about games suitable for the age level of the children, about mothers to help with the party, and about simple refreshments. When the party took place a few weeks later, Miss Frank and the principal of her school felt that she had not only arranged a memorable experience for the children, but that she had also built favorable rapport between a leading family of the community and the school.

Another teacher, Miss Young, felt that she needed to know something about what children in her classes had to work with at home. She felt that her conception of the homes of poorer children in her class probably differed from the reality of those homes. She realized that it was unrealistic to expect to know the families of even half of the large numbers of children in her room, but that she could get acquainted with a small sample of at least one or two families each semester. In a few years she would then build a clearer concept of their lives.

Miss Young looked up on a local map the streets where the least well dressed children lived. Then she arranged her time so that each Friday afternoon she could get her exercise by taking a walk through the district where they lived, a district in which she would feel unsafe at night but in which women and children went safely about their affairs by day.

For several weeks, Miss Young got acquainted with the life of the poor district, but not with the families of her children. However, her references to specific places in their neighborhood made school more interesting to the poorer children. Furthermore, they got used to the idea that Miss Young liked to go for a walk where they lived.

The Friday afternoon that Miss Young saw Mary minding her baby brother, she got into home life that she had never imagined. Fortunately she had changed to a pair of walking shoes and had put her gloves in her moneyless purse, thus reducing the social distance between herself and Mary's people. She was sincerely appreciative of Mary as a girl who liked school and did her best. She found it easy to sit down on the solid part of the porch step, ignore the baby's stained clothing, and enjoy the baby's smile. Presently she was in the kitchen talking about school with Mary's mother and using the folding pocketknife from her purse to help Mary's mother peel potatoes for supper.

Finishing her walk half an hour later, Miss Young was busy planning how to enlarge the pioneer unit in social studies to include meal preparation without the convenience of running water, the conservation of clothing by passing outgrown garments to younger children, and the necessity of schools to teach children how to mesh into an advancing civilization. She felt that she had increased the probability that Mary would stay in school because she had made school more understandable not only to Mary, but also to Mary's mother.

A principal of an elementary school in a metropolitan area reported an incident that illustrates the necessity for an administrator to have no trepidation about social distance between himself and families of his district:

A rather interesting and unexpected incident occurred this afternoon about ten minutes after school was out. A youngster came to say that a boy was waiting for him in order to beat him up after school. He was obviously upset about it, so I walked outside with him and saw him around the corner. As I waved goodbye to him, I turned around and noticed Marvin, one of our fifth-grade boys, about to light up a cigarette in his mouth. Obviously, he had not expected to see me out on the corner.

I asked Marvin where he lived. He said, "About a block and a half from here."

I said, "Come on. We'll walk on up to your house and see your mother."

He said, "I don't have a mother."

"Well," I said, "we'll talk to your father, then."

He said, "My father's at work."

I said, "Well, let's go on over, anyway, and talk to someone."

By the time we got near to the house, Marvin began to apologize for what I was going to find in the house. He said it was going to be untidy, unclean, and so on and so forth.

We went upstairs into an unkempt room. Clothing and shoes were strewn about the room; the bed, which was only a mattress, was unmade.

I asked Marvin who slept there. He said he and his father did, that they lived alone.

I asked him what time his father would be home.

"Not until three in the morning," he said.

"Well, who takes care of you then?" I asked.

"Nobody," he said. "I stay home alone."

I said that this did not seem right. Then I asked him what he was going to eat for dinner.

He said that there wasn't anything in the house, that his father

might come home about six o'clock, and that they would go out
to eat.

So I opened the refrigerator and looked in. There was nothing
in the refrigerator. I asked him where the cupboard was. He
showed me. There was nothing in the cupboard. There was not
one bite of food in the house.

I asked Marvin where his mother was. He said she had died.
With that he began to cry. I let him cry for a few minutes and
told him I was sorry that his mother had died.

"Do you want to talk about it?" I asked.

He said, "No."

At that point a young man about twenty-five or six years old
came up the stairs and said, "Hello."

I introduced myself, telling him who I was. I still had the
cigarette and matches in my hand. I asked him if he were the
boy's father.

He said, "No, I take care of Marvin."

I told him I really was not as concerned about Marvin smoking
as I was that he was going to be alone until three in the morning,
and that I had looked and had found no food in the house.

The man then became a little angry with Marvin and said,
"Why did you tell the principal that?"

He turned to me and explained that he and his wife took care
of the boy, that he ate with them, and that he stayed with them
when his father was away.

Hearing this, Marvin went into a regular temper tantrum
because his story had been found out.

About this time, the man's wife came up the stairs. She threw
her arms around the boy, and told her husband how mistreated he
had been and that he needed someone to take care of him. She
did not once reprimand him or try to pin him down on his story.

The husband motioned for me to come outside with him. There
he told me that he was on a ninety-day leave from the armed
services because his wife had had a nervous breakdown and was
under psychiatric care. Marvin, he said, was quite a troublemaker
around the neighborhood, cursing at adults, taking things, and so
on. As I left, I asked the man if he would tell Marvin's father that
I would like to see him and would appreciate having a conference
with him about Marvin and his problems.

I stumbled on this situation just by accident. The boy had been
in our school only about a month. I was not aware that he had any
problems, for he functioned normally in the classroom and on the
school grounds. But, by inadvertently catching him smoking, I
opened up a whole problem situation to work out with the boy's
father.

Teachers are interested in minimizing social distance between them-selves and parents. At the same time they need to use the concept of social distance to maximize the gap between the schools and irresponsible adults. For instance, schools of Casper, Wyoming, have worked with parents to make use of social distance to keep children unmolested.[5] Police Chief Danigan explained to volunteer watchers how to describe a person to be identified, and the importance of writing down at once the license number of a suspicious looking car. Superintendent of Schools Morris Griffin saw to it that the school children were taught such basic safety rules as:

Don't accept money, candy or gum from strangers.
Don't accept rides from strangers or accompany a stranger anywhere.

In increasing numbers of urban communities, placards are appearing that tell children where to find a "Block Parent" and a "Helping Hand."

Providing a Favorable Conference Setting

Decisions about when and where to confer with a parent are primarily decisions about how to provide a setting favorable for solving a problem. If a child's behavior shows that he has a problem, school personnel and parents endeavor to work out ways of helping him solve it. Or parents anticipate a problem and ask the help of the school in preventing its occurrence. Or the school sees a child headed for difficulty and tries to develop parental sensitivity to the problem and parental help in ob-viating it. All three of these situations call for objective and realistic discussion in a physical and social setting conducive to objectivity and realism. Good decisions about when and where to confer with a parent can make the difference between success and failure in helping a child solve his problems.

Arrangements for talking over a child's problem are easily made when parents and school personnel have a background of regular interaction, perhaps based on similar personal values held by middle-class people, perhaps developed through working together in the parent-teacher as-sociation or some community project. But conference arrangements re-quire more careful consideration when social distance is to be covered.

Having a plan for each family to interact with the school is a good basis for parent-school conferences of all kinds. If the school has arranged

5 Elaine Q. Barrow, "Helping Hands for Kids in Danger." *Parade,* April 25, 1965.

for each parent to talk with the teachers of his children at the convenience of the parent, then the school has set the stage for a parent conference which can be a single conference or the first of a series of conferences. By keeping track of the parents who accept the invitation and those who do not, the school can proceed to make individual arrangements with parents whose children need further help with the problems they face.

"Hello, Mrs. Smith," says Miss Van Doren when telephoning the mother of Clifford Smith, whose school behavior is not what she expects. After introducing herself, Miss Van Doren goes on to say: "In the fall each teacher has a conference with one or both parents about the progress his child is making at school. I so enjoy having Clifford in my group this year and am eager to talk with you about what he is doing. I have some of his work to show you and would like to tell you what boys and girls of his age do in our school. When is a convenient time for us to talk?"

If Mrs. Smith says that she cannot see Miss Van Doren at school, Miss Van Doren suggests seeing her at home. If Mrs. Smith says that she works during the hours after school, Miss Van Doren suggests a conference before school starts. If Mrs. Smith continues being negative about a conference, Miss Van Doren goes back to the general point that teachers and parents are both important in the life of a child and need to work together for his good. As soon as she gets agreement on this general point, Miss Van Doren asks Mrs. Smith to suggest a conference time and accepts her suggestion. If later she finds that she cannot possibly arrange to meet Mrs. Smith at that time, she can call Mrs. Smith and work out a substitute arrangement. The fact that Miss Van Doren is making a genuine effort to talk with her will persuade Mrs. Smith that she, too, should make an effort on behalf of her child. At the least, Miss Van Doren and Mrs. Smith can develop a telephone dialogue to help Clifford, and at best they can sit down together to discuss his problems.

The place designated for a parent conference should be attractive to parents. A bouquet of flowers helps to make an ordinary office into a pleasant room, and a well-appointed office can help produce a comfortable feeling. Of course, a sincere welcome by the person in charge and real help with problems are the essential factors in making the school a place to which parents like to come.

Privacy for an uninterrupted discussion is desirable in every conference setting. If a discussion can be interrupted at any time by the intrusion of a new personality, participants will be distracted and their mutual rapport interfered with. In general, if an audience situation develops, it is desirable to terminate either the audience situation or the parent conference by making arrangements to talk further at another time. Talking with a parent in the presence of an additional person restricts the conversational area to matters of concern to all the people present. This limitation may make the parent conference of little or no value in solving the child's problem.

If someone comes into the conference room, the school person can say to the parent, "Pardon me. It will take just a minute to clear this up." Such a remark tells the parent that he will have complete attention in just a few minutes, and tells the interrupter that he has only a minute of time for his problem. That minute can be used on the problem, or on setting another time for considering it. With the interruption taken care of for the time being, the school person can arrange to avoid further interruptions—perhaps by putting a sign on the door, saying, "Please come back at _____ o'clock." Then he can give his full attention to the parent conference.

Respecting Parental Emotions

To have objective and realistic discussions with parents about their children's problems is not always easy. Usually, a problem of a child is attributable, wholly or in part, to parental behavior. If parents were aware of the nature of this relation and interested in changing their ways for the benefit of their children, the children's problems would not exist. Parental reluctance in recognizing the actual problem of their child and in changing existing patterns of behavior is to be expected. So also are emotional reactions which grow out of parental involvement in the problems.

In order to minimize emotions that interfere with objectivity and realism, the wise school person arranges parent conferences so as to maximize the mild, pleasant emotions which enhance rapport and sustain constructive action to help children. If a parent comes into a conference emotionally disturbed, the school person may say, "You seem upset. Would another time be better for talking about your child's school work?" If the parent comes in looking discouraged or depressed, the school person finds something to praise realistically.

To get a conference started on an even emotional keel, it helps to give each parent a genuine and reassuring welcome. If a parent is concerned about his personal status in the school situation, or is fearful about conferring with school personnel, these concerns need to be allayed before the problem of the child can be dealt with effectively.

Deciding to Confer

Either a middle-class parent or a school person is apt to initiate a conference when a child's problems reach a point where adult help is needed. But parents of other social groups are apt to overlook or ignore their child's problems, or to depend on the school to advise them of the need for parents and school to work together for the good of the child.

Where casual contacts of the market place, club affairs, and community gatherings build rapport with parents, the problems of their children are easily discussed within a framework of mutual confidence. But where parents are from social groups distant from that of school people, school personnel must not only take the initiative in arranging a parent conference, but also in assuring that it will be an uninterrupted time for objective, realistic discussion of problems that a child faces or is apt to face if he continues his present patterns of behavior. In each conference that occurs, either by chance or by arrangement, mutual confidence and good rapport should be furthered.

_____Chapter Two_____

BUILDING AN
EFFECTIVE
RAPPORT
WITH PARENTS_____

Reporting pupil progress to parents is an accepted part of the school's function which affords regularly recurring opportunities for developing rapport with parents. A conscientious teacher gives a great deal of time and serious consideration to such reporting. Whatever method is used, oral or written, the teachers do much of the work required in reporting after school hours.

School systems use various written forms for a "report card." These are usually devised by a committee consisting of school personnel. Occasionally representatives selected from among the parents serve on such committees.

Many school systems are almost constantly in the process of revising the report card form which, in itself, shows that neither parents nor teachers are satisfied that an accurate and understandable appraisal of a child's work can be reduced to the categories and symbols used on the report card.

The most defensible of the report card forms used in elementary schools provides for coverage of the statutory school subjects and personality development, and uses a grading system that takes into consideration individual variations in ability.

School systems using only a report card for reporting pupil progress to parents, usually recognize that conferences between parents and teachers must be held in certain instances to solve acute learning or behavior problems.

Studies[1] have shown that teachers are generally enthusiastic in their attitudes concerning the value of conferences with parents but indicate some feelings of inadequacy about their ability to handle face-to-face contacts with parents effectively. Certain administrators are reluctant to have inexperienced teachers hold conferences with parents.

Obviously, if individual parent-teacher conferences are productive of better home and school relationships, an opportunity to learn how to conduct successful person-to-person conferences should be included in the professional education of prospective teachers in colleges and universities.

Many school districts give assistance to teachers in methods of holding conferences with parents.[2] The need for such in-service education is apparent if teachers who are new to the profession or who are inexperienced in the conference method are to fulfill this important function with skill, confidence and satisfaction.

In districts where great progress has been made in individual parent-teacher conferencing, parents often request that use of the formal report card be continued along with conferences. The use of both a report card and a face-to-face conference as the regular procedure for informing parents of their children's progress represents an investment of a considerable portion of the teacher's time.

Can teachers do both? Should they be expected to do both? Surveys of parent groups indicate that parents overwhelmingly favor conferences but want a report card also. Each school district should face the issue of the best use of the teacher's time. If a dual system of reporting means using time which the teacher should devote to the preparation necessary for guiding the learning of children, then serious consideration should be given to simplifying the written report and reducing the number of times it is issued.

The major responsibility of teachers is the guidance of children. The regular use of two methods of reporting encroaches upon the time and energy of teachers which should be devoted to the important task of teaching.

[1] Helen Heffernan and Lorene E. Marshall, "Reporting Pupil Progress in California Cities," *California Journal of Elementary Education,* XXIV (November, 1955) 67–77.
[2] See Chapter Ten.

Report Cards vs. Parent-Teacher Conferences

Martha C. Johnson, a mother and teacher, says:

> . . . reports are useful if they tell parents how their child is progressing in absorbing the values, facts and skills urged upon him each day. Further, reports should tell parents how they can help a child attain wisdom and inner strength.[3]

On the other hand, Mrs. Johnson is fearful of the effect on children and parents in some instances. She says:

> The most telling objection to the usual form of report card is the lethal use to which parents may put it. Most parents genuinely admire their children, until the school seems to suggest the parents may be wasting their affections on second-rate products.

Parents may act on the information received on a report card, or even in a parent-teacher conference, in a variety of negative ways. They may:

- Bribe the child with hard cash for high marks, or withhold allowances for low marks.
- Scold or punish him because he did not receive as high a mark as another child in the class.
- Deny him a trip or a pleasure he prizes highly.

The outcome of such practices is that the child may develop an unfortunate attitude toward learning—money becomes more important than the precious knowledge learned. The child learns to learn for a reward, to secure parental approval, or to escape punishment, and not because of interest in and curiosity about the subject being studied. When the reward is no longer forthcoming and the punishment no longer to be feared, the individual will loathe learning and do as little of it as possible. In a world changing as rapidly as the contemporary world, this is a disastrous outcome, since the only hope of intellectual survival is dedication to life-long learning.

Mrs. Johnson comments further:

[3] Martha C. Johnson, "Let's Get Rid of Report Card Jitters," *Parent's Magazine*, V. 37, Pt. 1 (June, 1962), 40–41.

Then, too, there is the damage . . . to the slow or average child. . . . The less successful student can feel humiliated and defeated by poor report cards, even if his parents assure him that he is loved for himself and not for his marks. Here lies the great conflict between new psychological insight and old educational practice.

We all agree that too many children become anxious adults because of adult disapproval in their youth. We also know that a child's estimate of his own worth is based on the attitudes and judgments of the adults in his world. Yet we hand him official looking documents which he can interpret as meaning, "I'm no good!" It's true that under this pressure some children may work harder and may learn more facts, but, in the long run, this kind of competition is unlikely to encourage genuine growth in mind or spirit.

According to Mary and Lawrence K. Frank the report card

> . . . rates in inflexible terms the child's abilities and achievements. Conscientious parents feel themselves responsible if the card indicates failure; it seems somehow to imply a negligence of their own in not making the child study harder. And so the child is scolded and punished, made to promise to do better. . . .[4]

Parent-teacher conferences were originally planned to break this rigidity—to bring parents and teachers into face-to-face intimate contact. In such a situation parents find that

> . . . along with his difficulties, their child also has potentialities and abilities of which they are unaware. They will often discover that, with the teacher's cooperation and with some extra attention to the child's problem at home, they may be able to effect a change in his behavior in school and perhaps avoid a learning problem later on.[5]

And again, these perceptive students of human growth and development advise that

> . . . the most helpful kind of report for parents, even when written monthly reports are sent home, is the conference with the teacher. Not only is it a give-and-take of information, full of

[4] Lawrence K. and Mary Frank, *How to Help Your Child in School,* New York: The Viking Press, 1950, p. 3.
[5] *Ibid.,* p .5.

specific observations and examples, but it is also the best way for teachers to tell parents about the aims of their programs.[6]

Unfortunately, reports are not always favorable either on the formal report card or in the informal conference. All children have problems in growing up. The Franks suggest that in discussing a discouraging report with a child a parent might say

> This isn't a case of loving you less because of marks. But it wouldn't help if we threw the report card away either, because you'd know and we'd know you were just dodging the issue. You have wonderful capacities, and, like all human beings, you have difficulties too. Where do you need help? This is your task, but we're here to help you. It's a good idea to know now where your weak spots are in school work and be on the lookout for places where you have to make extra effort. It's difficult and very tough going, it's true, especially in those places where you try hardest. . . . Just let's be honest with ourselves. Difficulties are usually easier to meet when we know *where* they are and *why* they are there.

To provide children with guidance of this quality, the parent is better equipped following a well-planned parent-teacher conference in which the parent is free to ask for further elucidation on any subject under discussion and thus to understand its significance in terms of the child's potential.

A Foundation for Individual Conferences

When the personnel of a school district decides to follow the sound advice of experienced educators and psychologists and substitute individual parent-teacher conferences for other means of reporting pupil progress, teachers are confronted with the question of how to establish the good rapport essential for a successful conference.

The individual conference should be preceded by a number of activities which have proved successful in cementing home-school relationships. These may have included home visits by the teacher, parent visits and observations in the classroom, grade level group meetings to discuss the characteristics of children of this maturity level and the learning experiences the school provides for them, group meetings to discuss the common developmental problems that children encounter in growing up, and the

[6] *Ibid.,* p. 313.

operation of a small library with books, pamphlets and magazines of special interest to parents.

Home visits.   All home visits should be scheduled in advance of the visit in order to give the mother an opportunity to be ready to welcome her child's teacher. Visits by teachers are for the purpose of getting acquainted and of fostering happy relationships.

To make a success of the home visit the teacher should genuinely appreciate the role of the parents. She should realize that most parents are doing the best they can in terms of insights, motivations, and aspirations. The parents were the child's first teachers and they recall what a slow process learning often was. Parents usually realize that the teacher has a difficult job, that she has a genuine concern for the child's welfare and that her purpose for visiting the home is to develop working relationships with the parents. Most parents know that a child's needs can be most adequately met when his home and school environments are brought into a harmonious, supporting relationship. The education of a child demands a full partnership representing the significant adults in his life.

Parent observations.   Early in the school year, many schools issue an urgent invitation for parents to visit and observe their child at work in the school situation.

In a brochure entitled *Teamwork Does It*,[7] the California Congress of Parents and Teachers suggests six rules of classroom etiquette regarding a parent's visit to a classroom. These suggestions are immeasurably helpful to a parent who feels a little awkward about school visiting:

1. Help the teacher to feel secure about your first visit. Send her a note or call her and ask if a certain day would be a good time to come. . . .
2. Try to arrive during a recess period so your entrance will be unobtrusive.
3. Don't expect the teacher to take time during class to discuss the individual child.
4. Take a seat in the back of the room.
5. Observe impersonally what is going on; children are sensitive to audience reaction.
6. Find something to praise about the class and make this comment to the teacher upon leaving.

[7] *Teamwork Does It.* Los Angeles: California Congress of Parents and Teachers, Suite 300, 322 West Twenty-first Street, n.d., Single copies 5¢.

The planned observation early in the school year is an excellent time for interpreting the program to the parents, for discussing the children's personal development, and for setting forth educational goals for the year.

What each parent observes varies from parent to parent. For many mothers, it is enough to see the physical setting her child is in, and to see what the teacher is like. Such mothers attend open house at school and open house where their husbands work because they know it is usual for mothers to carry on these activities. As mothers, they feel important in visibly supporting the members of their family before the eyes of the community.

Parents, especially those attending a demonstration at school for the first time, are eager to be a good audience. They are reassured when school people express appreciation for their quiet listening and thank them for their interest in their school and their children's education.

The skillful teacher can guide parent observations at the same time that she guides the children by pointing out what each child is to do. For instance, when parents are observing a beginning program in Spanish presented by television and followed by classroom instruction, the teacher may say:

> Boys and girls, we are happy to have your parents visiting us this afternoon. They have come to share our Spanish lesson, and will listen as quietly as we do to our television teacher.
>
> What season of the year is it? In English, what are some of the words that we use to describe this season? . . .
>
> Our television teacher will tell us some of the Spanish words we can use to describe this season. Listen carefully to what she says so that each of us can talk about the season with Spanish words.

Alerted by such teacher cues, visiting parents will watch how the children in the class, and especially their own child, handles the learning problem. Some parents may follow up the teaching at school with practice at home. Some may comment to their child, or to his teacher, about what he did in the class time. Others may remain passive observers, but will have greater understanding and appreciation of what the school is trying to do.

Grade level group meetings. Many schools arrange for grade-level group meetings of parents enrolled in each classroom. Group meetings are particularly valuable to conserve time in giving general information about the school's program and policies. Group meetings are also useful in enlisting parent's cooperation on school problems.

Parents have much to contribute in the field of family life education and any effective program must have their co-operation. They should be consulted concerning sex and other social education topics and be asked to approve the use of books and films. When this is done in advance, there is seldom criticism. Many parents gain assurance from the discovery that other parents in the group have had many of the same problems with which they are faced. Suggestions from various parents as to what they have tried successfully may motivate other parents to try better courses of action. The gradual development of personal relationships that take place in repeated group discussions furthers parent rapport at the same time that it helps parents to become effective participants in group discussions.

A library for parents.   Another contribution to the development of rapport is provision for a small, specialized library of books, pamphlets, and magazines of interest to parents. Although much material directed to parents appears in current magazines, important publications based on sound research can easily be missed by parents in their general reading. Comments by school people help parents select good educational material in line with the needs and interests of their family.

In any school system where preliminary steps have been taken to enlist the participation and involvement of parents in the school, the task of inaugurating individual conferences is greatly simplified. The teacher who has already met many parents in group meetings is ready for conferences with them, especially if they have visited her classroom as well. The teacher then will greet the parent who comes for a conference as a respected friend. She will show by her gracious greeting that she welcomes the parent and anticipates valuable outcomes from the time they can spend together.

What to Discuss with Parents

Nearly all parents want to know how their children are progressing in their school subjects and how they compare with other children of their age and grade. Many parents are concerned about their children's personality development and how well they get along with other children and the adults they encounter at school. The judgment of the teacher is valued by parents interested in the special talents and abilities of their children. Equally, parents are concerned with obstacles which seem to block a child's achievement of his maximum potential. These are the factors a teacher must be prepared to discuss with parents wisely and sympathetically.

Achievement in school subjects. Although many elementary schools organize the curriculum in terms of broad, integrated areas of human experience in which the separate subjects receive less emphasis, many parents are accustomed to thinking in terms of discrete content fields.

In discussing the various subjects the teacher may find useful the following specific items related to the different subject-matter fields:

READING

Understands what he reads
Works to develop independent reading habits
Enjoys reading books at his reading level

WRITING

Expresses himself well
Uses basic writing skills
Writes legibly
Spells correctly
Uses good sentence structure
Learns to use new words

ORAL EXPRESSION

Works to express himself effectively
Works to increase his vocabulary
Listens carefully and reproduces what he has heard accurately
Is growing in recognition of the importance of correct use of language

MATHEMATICS

Knows mathematical facts
Understands arithmetic processes
Applies skill in solving problems

SOCIAL STUDIES

Works to develop a knowledge and understanding of home, community, state, nation, and world
Works to develop skill in the use of materials: many books, newspapers, magazines, maps, atlas, encyclopedia

	Is growing in sound social understanding and attitudes
SCIENCE	Works to develop keen powers of observation
	Works to apply scientific method in experimentation and inquiry
	Is growing in scientific knowledge
HEALTH AND PHYSICAL EDUCATION	Works to develop and practice good health habits
	Helps to maintain safety in school and playground
	Plays and enjoys games
	Works to develop skills in physical education
	Is growing in his knowledge of health and safety
MUSIC	Takes part happily in group singing
	Responds to rhythm and participates freely in rhythmical activities
	Works to develop basic music skills
ART	Expresses ideas creatively
	Works to develop skills with a variety of media
	Is growing in appreciation of the products of artistic creators

In the discussion with parents the teacher will, of course, select and adapt specific items to the maturity level of the child. Obviously, all these items cannot be considered in one conference, but it is important that the teacher regularly emphasize a well-balanced curriculum in the education of children. In choosing subjects to discuss, the teacher must be careful that no prestige value is given to one aspect of human development over another. The royal road to self-realization and self-confidence for one child may be mathematics or science; for another, it may be music, art, creative writing, or leadership in the solution of social problems. The world needs competent people with a wide variety of talents. The conference should help parents to value the strengths a child possesses even if these differ widely from the fields of human endeavor favored by the parent.

Personality development.   The teacher must give thoughtful consideration to her comments on a child's developing personality. Important as are the curriculum of the school and the achievement of children in attaining curricular goals, the major responsibility of the teacher is the guidance of all phases of a child's development—physical, mental, social, and emotional. Every human being is a unitary organism with all aspects of his development occurring simultaneously. Parents sometimes say, "If the school will take care of our child's intellectual development, we will take care of all other aspects of his development." Fortunately, the child cannot be fragmented in this fashion. The "mental child" cannot come to school and leave the physical, social, or emotional child at home. He is not separable into parts and so his education must always be a joint enterprise in which home, school, community, or any institution in the community which influences him must participate in every possible way in advancing his interests and welfare.

The teacher may find these questions useful in deciding upon subjects to discuss regarding a child's personality:

- Is he developing a variety of interests?
- Is he usually courteous and considerate?
- Does he respect the rights and property of others?
- Does he share his out-of-school experiences?
- Does he share his skills and available materials with others?
- Does he accept his fair share of responsibility?
- Does he carry tasks through to completion?
- Does he work to the best of his ability?
- Does he give evidence of creative ability?

Frequently, parents want to know how their child compares with other children in the class. The teacher must use his best judgment about responding to such a question in terms of the probable effect of his statement on the child's relationship with his parents. Will he be subjected to pressure to achieve beyond his capacity? Will he be rejected by his parents? No one can advise a teacher precisely what to say, but the teacher can always say, in effect:

> The measurement instruments now available to us in education are not sufficiently precise to answer your question accurately.

Your son is achieving at the level of expectancy we have for him on the basis of the information we are now able to obtain about his capacity and interests. With your loving and supportive encouragement at home, appropriate to his apparent ability, he will make progress. Each individual is different from every other individual and comparisons are, therefore, not fruitful. Our concern about *every* child is that *he* realize *his* potential.

At no time should a teacher be surprised into a comparison between two children in a class. The information the teacher has about any child is privileged. He must use his best judgment as to how much of this information he believes he can safely share with a child's parents. When such information is shared with any other lay person, who may question only from motives of idle or even malicious curiosity, it becomes *gossip* and has no place in the intimate professional relationship every good teacher has with his pupils.

The teacher is constantly aware of each child's special strengths and talents or weaknesses and disabilities. This knowledge may be shared with parents but only when the teacher is in a position to make positive and constructive suggestions of ways to enhance the strengths or lessen the weaknesses.

The teacher must invest a considerable amount of time in planning each individual conference so it will have maximum benefit for the child and the parents as well as the school. The more careful the preparation by the teacher the more successful will be the outcomes in improved home-school relationships, in making school experiences highly profitable for the child and in solving problems before they become so acute that they have a detrimental effect on the child's development.

When a parent has a genuine interest in knowing how his child behaves in school, the teacher can encourage him in visiting his child's class and observing his behavior in some detail. Here is a set of questions[8] which one school provided for parents to use as a guide to their observations. Part, or occasionally all of it, might be given to a parent, depending upon his skill as an observer.

PARENTS' GUIDE TO OBSERVATION

1. a. Is the child enjoying himself?
   b. What is indicated by his facial expression?
   c. How interested is he in what is going on?

[8] *Ibid.*

2. a. What are his relationships with others in the group?
   b. With the teacher?
   c. Do they like and enjoy each other?
   d. How cooperative are they?
   e. How relaxed and at ease are they with each other? With the other children?
   f. Does he take the lead in doing things with others?
   g. Does he help others in carrying out their ideas?
   h. How frequently and under what circumstances does he seem

Shy?	Assured?	Uncooperative?	Cooperative?
Timid?	Confident?	Quarrelsome?	Agreeable?
Selfish?	Generous?	Aggressive?	Withdrawing?

3. a. How active is he? When is he active? When is he passive?
   b. Is he busy or just sitting?
   c. Is he busy at the same things as the others, or following his own interests?
   d. How purposeful is his activity—does he complete his projects?
4. a. How does he solve his problems?
   b. Does he try to work them out for himself?
   c. Does he go to the teacher for help?
   d. Does he seek to enlist the cooperation of other children?
   e. How readily does he give up?
   f. Does he resort to tears or temper when frustrated?
5. What is he learning?

Democratic Attitudes in Home and School

As important facets of a nation that is a democracy, both home and school have responsibility for developing future citizens for the nation. Ernest G. Osborne[9] says that homes in which parents adhere to democratic principles and ideals are characterized by these four attitudes:

1. The freedom given a child to make progressively more significant decisions concerning his own welfare;

[9] Ernest G. Osborne, *Democracy Begins in the Home*. Public Affairs Pamphlet No. 192, 153. New York: Public Affairs Committee, p. 4.

2. The respect shown for his uniqueness;
3. The understanding of his particular needs and how they may be fulfilled;
4. Cooperative effort in seeking the individual and mutual satisfactions both parents and children desire.

Many parents are confident that they practice these behaviors with their children but at the same time they believe that it is their job as experienced adults to make all the decisions. Frequently, too, parents demand that children achieve what they have neither the maturity nor readiness to do, thus disregarding the fact that each child is a unique human being growing according to his own growth pattern. Sometimes parents overlook the fact that an individual may find many different ways to satisfy his needs and achieve his developmental tasks. In far too many families "cooperation" means doing what the parents wish the child to do, and the child is judged "uncooperative" if he has ideas which run contrary to parental judgment.

This wide gap between the democratic behavior the parent believes is characteristic of his behavior in day-by-day situations may have its counterpart for the teacher working with a group of children. All adults, parents and teachers, need constantly to be reminded that democratic attitudes in their relationships with children are a step toward achieving the highest form of life and government that mankind has yet devised.

Democratic attitudes in day-by-day relationships free children emotionally to be and do their best. A child growing up in such a climate has a positive self-image. He knows he is wanted, respected, and loved in his home and school. And because this is true he is free to love and respect others, and to accept them as different but interesting and desirable human beings.

Parental and School Pressures

In a grim report by James Jan-Tausch, Director of Remedial Education, the New Jersey State Department of Education released the story: *Suicide of Children, 1960–63.*[10] During the three-year period covered by the report, forty-one students, ranging in age from seven through nineteen committed suicide; nine were girls. Eight of these children lived

[10] James Jan-Tausch, *Suicide of Children 1960–1963, New Jersey Public School Students.* Trenton: Office of Special Education Services, Department of Education, 1964.

in large cities, nine in suburban or small cities, and twenty-four in rural or semi-rural areas. The investigator expressed the conviction that at least an equal number of deaths were reported as accidental to protect the family. He further states his conviction that nine serious attempts at suicide are made and fail for every one that succeeds.

Because of the absence of effective records it was difficult for the investigator to arrive at specific causes. The reader concludes that the causes are similar to those reported by Don D. Jackson, as follows:

1. Feelings of rejection by significant adult authority figures
2. Inability to form close, confiding relationships with adults or peers
3. Failure to achieve membership in a socially approved group.[11]

The median child in this New Jersey group of forty-one was between 14 and 15 years of age, white, Protestant, oldest child in family, lived in home with both parents, normal intelligence, poor academic achievement, average reader, engaged in no extra-curricular activities, had no close friends, had no special skills, was in good health, and showed hostility through aggression or withdrawal.

Obviously, this "median child" had many assets as well as some serious problems. Had the "significant adult authority figures"—parents and teachers—met two or three times a year for discussion of this child's school progress, surely as men and women of good will they could have found ways and means to help him solve his problems.

Many activities now going on in schools give evidence of the desire of school personnel to provide better individual guidance for children and to improve communication with the homes they serve. A nationwide trend to provide opportunity for parent-teacher conferences increases confidence that reciprocal relationships will contribute effectively to the achievement of each child's potential.

[11] Don D. Jackson, "Suicide," *Scientific American*, 191, No. 5, (November, 1954) pp. 88–96.

Chapter Three

CONDUCTING A
SUCCESSFUL
CONFERENCE_____ .

Successful conferences between parents and school people grow out of an understanding of factors important in the development of children. Parents and teachers are mutually concerned about helping the child to learn the knowledge, skills, and attitudes essential to successful living. They are mutually concerned about helping the child to grow up to be a socially and emotionally mature person. Concerned thus with common purposes, the social distance they frequently maintain between them should be reduced to a minimum.

When fears of either parents or teachers intrude, conferences suffer. But when common goals of family and school are emphasized and the conference is kept centered on the good of the child, much is accomplished to further the development of the child.

Basic Understandings

Over a period of years, a child sets out for elementary school nearly every morning. If he dislikes school, he may develop all sorts of reasons and excuses for not going, thus creating a daily conflict that is not conducive to his own or his family's happiness. If this attitude persists, he is likely to join the ranks of the dropouts who face bleak adult lives in a society that has "no room at the bottom." Learning is closely related to attitudes. A child will learn most effectively what he wants to learn.

The more he enjoys school, the more alert and receptive he will be to learning experiences.

Parents and teachers have the power largely to determine what the child's attitude toward school will be. It is, therefore, of the greatest importance that parents and teachers work closely together, develop positive attitudes toward each other, maintain positive relationships, and arrive at goals upon which they agree.

Certain negative factors have hindered the development of positive attitudes toward the school and positive relationships between parents and teachers. Parents and teachers have both failed to recognize that educating a child is a task they have in common. The home has been thought of as the place where children were reared by their parents, the school as the place where children were educated by their teachers. Parents' unconscious fear of, and hostility toward, the authoritarian teacher and school was often the result of their own unfortunate experiences in childhood. Too frequently the school of the past was not geared to child interest and level of development, and it produced an adult who was not concerned about the school.

Cooperation is steadily improving, but remnants of fear and lack of understanding still interfere with mutual accomplishment by parents and teachers.

Parents' fears.   Some parents fear teachers. Sometimes their fears grow out of feelings that they are not as well educated as the teacher and that he will think them uninformed if they ask questions. Their fear of the teacher may be an unconscious carry-over from their own childhood. Sometimes they fear that they may be considered "meddlers," "trouble makers," "apple polishers." They fear that any criticism might lead to reprisals against their child. They fear that they are being blamed because their child acts as a normal child and not as a superior adult. They fear that the school may be experimenting with their child and may leave him unprepared to meet the demands of a complex world.

Teachers' fears.   Some teachers fear parents. In the past, teachers have had conferences only with irritated parents who came to school because of a "problem" and these experiences have generated fear. Overworked teachers fear that individual parent conferences and work with the parent-teacher association will result in an insuperable work load. Young teachers fear parents who are older and more experienced persons than themselves and older teachers fear the limited sensitivity and inexperienced judgment of youthful parents. Teachers fear they may not be able satisfactorily to answer parents' questions about a child's problem. Teachers fear that parents may be critical of their method of handling children.

Facing the issue.   The only solution to these problems of mutual fear and distrust is opportunity to face up to these issues openly in joint discussions. If the child is to have a positive attitude toward school, parents and teachers must have a positive attitude toward each other. This can exist only when they feel mutual respect for each other as persons and for the importance of the role each plays in the life of a developing personality. Both must start with the assumption that each is doing his best in guiding the child's learning experiences. Each must accept the fact that parents and teachers fall short of perfection and that both need, and will be greatly benefited by, the support of the other. This mutual support also gives the child an increased stability and security.

Both parents and teachers should appreciate the important role of the other in training and teaching the child. Teachers should recognize that the child spends at least three times as many of his waking hours under the supervision of his parents as he does at school. To the degree, therefore, that the teacher can help the parent to improve relationship with the child and make these hours a more creative and vital learning experience, the greater the benefit to the child, the parent, and the teacher. The parents should realize that the school is not merely a place where their child has his mind developed, but also a place where he may have experiences several hours each day of a type seldom available even in the best home; a place where he has the opportunity to participate as one of a group of children under competent teacher guidance. In school the children are guided through one learning experience to another by a teacher with creative ability. Concomitantly, the child is learning to adjust to the group, learning to cooperate, learning to listen and to follow directions. He discovers what may well be the greatest value of his school experience—the deep satisfaction that comes through group living.

In the past, parents and teachers have sought each other out and conferred only when confronted with a problem. In the regularly scheduled parent conference, parents and teachers have an opportunity to discuss ways in which they can help each other to help the child. They learn to know and appreciate each other. If the parents know the teacher, they are not so likely to accept a child's distorted report of what happened at school, and if the teacher knows the parents, he, too, can be more understanding. The friendship of parents and teachers gives the child a sense of confidence and security.

Common goals.   The parent conference affords opportunity for parents and teachers to arrive at common goals appropriate to the child's stage of development. The full development of the child is the basic concern of both parents and teachers. The home can no longer be the place where the child's physical needs alone are cared for and the school the place where only his intellectual needs are met. Both home and school are concerned with all aspects of the child's development.

The normally happy and healthy child desires to learn and the child who is enjoying his relationship with the teacher and with other children will enjoy the learning experiences which they share. In this connection, it is important for parents to recognize that play is the work of childhood and that the child who plays well with other children is on the way to working well with others at successive stages of development.

Parents are eager for their children to be successful in school and are usually eager to cooperate with the school. For the child, it is desirable that his home and school environments be harmonious. The child is adaptable and will respond quickly to an improved environment at home or school. The importance of this is apparent because it is easier to prevent than to cure problems.

General Purposes of Parent Conferences

The general purposes of parent-teacher conferences may be briefly summarized as follows:

1. *To enable the home and school to meet the needs of the child most effectively.*
2. *To establish a working relationship with parents in the interests of the child.*
3. *To assure a two-way communication between home and school.*
4. *To share with parents what is known about the growth characteristics and needs of specific age groups.*
5. *To share with parents the educational program which has been based on these growth characteristics and designed to meet the needs of children.*

6. *To help parents to understand the role of education in a democratic society.*

7. *To suggest ways parents can help children succeed in school.*

8. *To arrive at common objectives for the child at home and at school.*

9. *To interpret to parents their child's growth and progress in his school work.*

10. *To share with parents professional knowledge about social and emotional development of children.*

11. *To help the teacher acquire understanding of the child's relationship to his parents, brothers and sisters, and other family members.*

12. *To help the teacher to understand the family's aspirations for the child, his routines, interests, out-of-school activities, and the emotional tone of his home.*

13. *To provide opportunity for the teacher to perceive the parents' reaction to the school.*

14. *To help parents recognize the individual parent-teacher conference as an indispensable part of a modern educational program.*

Effective parent-teacher conferences can have far-reaching values in increased parental understanding of children, in appreciation of the educational program, and in the recognition of the role of the school in a democratic society. Reciprocally, teachers benefit through knowledge of the home environment from which the child comes, the ambitions of the parents for their children, as well as from increased cooperation in meeting the needs of the child, the school, and the community.

Individual Conferences with Children

A teacher should have frequent individual conferences with each child to appraise his efforts and his difficulties. This type of teacher-pupil conference may well be held prior to the parent-teacher conference. Children can be critical of their efforts if they feel that the effort is worthwhile, noted, and appreciated. When a child has the security of knowing where he is good, he can usually accept the fact that there are some things he needs to work on to do better.

A person-to-person conference with the child prior to the parent-teacher conference is reassuring to the child and frequently enlightening to the teacher. The child comes to understand the teacher's motives in discussing his progress with his parents. He realizes that this conference will not be an opportunity for reprisal for previous unacceptable behavior or failure to achieve. The teacher can discover what difficulties the child sees as insurmountable. Sometimes, the child himself can put his finger precisely on the spot where help is needed. He frequently reflects parental attitudes toward specific problems, so the teacher understands the necessity of a diplomatic approach to problems emotionally charged.

If the teacher keeps an informal record of these individual teacher-pupil conferences, the discussions can be sequentially built on previous topics. The child sees the serious nature of the teacher's individual guidance and the necessity of giving his best effort to the problems the teacher considers significant. As a child makes progress, the teacher can use the individual conference to congratulate the child on gains made toward self-realization. Such recognition is a tremendous stimulus to greater effort. The wise teacher knows that much of his success is measured in terms of his ability to give approval for the kind of behavior he wishes to promote.

Plan Parent Conference in Advance

Since the time a teacher can devote to conferring with each parent is necessarily limited to twenty or thirty minutes, except in most unusual cases, the teacher must design the conference carefully in advance, have clear purposes in mind, and perhaps set down the outcomes or goals expected from each particular conference.

Joseph P. Rice[1] suggested that in the advanced planning, teachers should answer such questions as these:

1. *Who should attend the conference and why?*
2. *What are limits within which discussion should be kept?*
3. *What are the main observations concerning a child that need to be brought to the attention of parents?*

[1] Joseph P. Rice, Jr., "The Importance of Parent-Teacher Conferences," *Education*, Vol. 83 (September, 1962), pp. 43–5.

4. *What tentative plans has the teacher arrived at for dealing with a child's particular problem?*
5. *At what point will it become obvious that no further good can come from the conference and that it should therefore be brought to a close?*

With regard to the first question, Dr. Rice says the parent-teacher conference will usually involve one or both parents or the child's guardian and the teacher. However, for particular reasons, it may be desirable to involve the principal, the school nurse, the psychologist, the guidance counselor or other members of the professional staff. Their role is to reinforce the teacher or to interpret technical information significant to the child's development.

A difference of opinion exists concerning the advisability of having the child participate in the conference. Younger children usually have little interest in attending a parent-teacher conference. Older children frequently say, "If I am to be discussed at a conference, I think I have a right to be there." Since nothing damaging to the child will ever be under discussion, this point of view seems quite defensible.

With regard to the second question about the limits of a discussion, the conference should always focus on the child; his strengths, his needs, and suggestions for his betterment involving the cooperative effort of home and school.

The third question deals with the main observations concerning a child that need to be brought to the attention of parents. These depend upon the individual child. Among the observations which merit attention are any unexplained change in performance or marked deviations above or below expected performance in

1. School subjects
2. Attitudes toward school
3. Behavior toward other children
4. School and playground activities.

The teacher brings to the conference samples of the child's work, scores on standardized tests, and anecdotal records of behavior. These types of data provide objective evidence which parents can see for themselves. Some teachers keep monthly samples of each child's work, and when these are spread out seriatim before the parent, he can see for himself evidence of improvement or deterioration. The parent notes what the school is trying to do and sees more clearly the successes or difficulties the child is encountering. Any sudden deterioration in behavior, prolonged moods of indifference or depression, lack of zest in activities and relationships previously enjoyed are symptomatic of a problem that merits investigation to find ways to remove the cause or causes. Any sudden improvement is evidence of a desirable input to be encouraged and continued.

As the teacher thinks about an individual child and his needs, he inevitably develops tentative plans. He may hypothesize that the cause of apathy in school is due to intense absorption in long TV sessions at night. He may guess that parents are comparing the child unfavorably to an older and more gifted brother. He may wonder whether school work is in competition with a plethora of out-of-school activities or with some absorbing interest in a subject placed elsewhere in the school curriculum. He may guess that the child's reading ability is insufficient to cope with the extensive reading requirements in the social studies program. As soon as the teacher has identified factors that may be related to a child's difficulty, he is well on the way to some tentative plans for solutions.

Finally, when the problem has been presented and time for discussion has been allowed, the conference should move forward briskly to mutually agreed upon plans for next steps at home and at school to improve the situation. The teacher can terminate the conference with a summary of the decisions reached and warm assurance of interest in the child and confidence in the belief that home and school working together faithfully can bring about a more successful adjustment.

Dr. Rice[2] lists the following as typical reasons for holding parent-teacher conferences:

- *To discuss reasons why a child is not working up to his potential*
- *To explore causes for discipline problems*
- *To discuss various adjustment problems*
- *To discuss factors that may be related to recent deterioration in work habits on the part of the pupil*
- *To identify and find help for any lack of ability a pupil may have.*

[2] *Ibid.*, p. 43.

Every successful conference reflects the teacher's ability in guiding human relationships. The focus of *every* conference should always be on the child. The parents should be immediately reassured of the teacher's sincere interest, affection, and appreciation of the child. The growing up process is a rugged one; no one escapes without confronting and solving problems.

The teacher avoids a defensive attitude or tone of voice. No case is being made against the child. Parents have feelings of guilt about any of their child's shortcomings and guilt is frequently expressed in hostile reactions. The teacher who works daily with thirty children may be able to achieve an objective attitude toward them. But the parent, closely identified with his own child, must of necessity be subjective. He will "stand up for his child" as if he were himself being attacked. And this is right and proper. The child must know this security, protection, and unfailing support. And so, the teacher must convince the parent that while the child is in school the teacher is in *locus parentis* and is on the side of the child just as the parents are.

The teacher who can bring to the parent-teacher conference a genuine affection for people, who has the ability "to stand in the shoes" of the parent, who is sympathetic to the child striving to grow up in a difficult world, will achieve the rapport essential to understanding and cooperation. Above all the teacher must maintain perspective, a sense of humor, and an optimistic belief that the problem is soluble if all interested people work together.

A Report of a Parent-Teacher Conference

The day for Mrs. Robinson's conference with Timmy's teacher had arrived. Ever since the appointment was made Mrs. Robinson had been thinking about this meeting. When she enrolled Timmy, she talked for a few minutes with Miss Franklin but there were forms to fill out and she was eager to get back to Baby Robert, who had been left with a neighbor.

Mrs. Robinson remembered with pleasure the group meeting of mothers during the second week of school. She enjoyed examining the equipment and instructional materials in the kindergarten room and the adjoining playyard which was reserved exclusively for the kindergarten children. This had relieved a nagging anxiety about how Timmy would manage to get along with the older children. Mrs. Robinson was impressed by what Miss Franklin told the group about the various kinds of learning experiences which would be provided during the year. She resolved to accept Miss Franklin's urgent invitation to spend an hour or two visiting the kindergarten while it was in session, but with Baby Robert's teeth making him so uncomfortable she was reluctant to ask her friendly neighbor to care for him while she visited Timmy's school.

For some unaccountable reason, Mrs. Robinson was nervous. What would Miss Franklin say about Timmy? Timmy was so eager to do things well (like his father) that sometimes he did not want to try to do new things—it was weeks before he ventured to ride the new bicycle his grandfather had been so happy to get for him. It was true that sometimes play sessions with neighbor children ended in fights. And, of course, Timmy exasperated her at times by his dawdling. No amount of urging got him dressed quickly and meals were a constant scene because he took so long to eat his food. Then—fortunately, it didn't happen often— Timmy was sometimes destructive. His mother was truly distressed about the time Timmy stamped on the big yellow duck that Baby Robert loved to play with in his bath. "At times, I guess I am a completely inadequate mother," sighed Mrs. Robinson. "I wonder what Miss Franklin will say about Timmy."

The clock had reached the exact minute when Mrs. Robinson must leave for her appointment. "Well, fortunately, no one else will be there," she thought, "I couldn't bear to have Big Tim hear what a wretched failure I have been with Timmy. But he is a darling, too," she murmured stoutly and inconsistently. "I hope Miss Franklin likes him."

A warm welcome.   Mrs. Robinson turned the knob on the kindergarten door and was greeted by a warm friendly smile as Miss Franklin came to meet her. "You are Mrs. Robinson, Timmy's mother, and I am so happy to see you again. Timmy is my right-hand man in kindergarten. You have certainly taught him to be a *very* helpful little boy."

Mrs. Robinson visibly relaxed and dropped into a comfortable chair to which Miss Franklin had pointed.

"How about coffee?" asked Miss Franklin. "Too soon after lunch?"

"Yes, I would love it, I think I must have forgotten lunch," said Mrs. Robinson.

An informal setting.   In a moment, coffee was poured and a plate of wafers appeared on a small table at Mrs. Robinson's elbow. Mrs. Robinson felt she had always known Miss Franklin, and between sips of coffee she poured out all her concerns about Timmy. She even mentioned the destruction of the baby's duck.

Listening. Miss Franklin listened quietly, replenished the coffee cups, helped herself to a wafer and pushed the plate in invitation closer to Mrs. Robinson.

Finally, Mrs. Robinson stopped almost breathless with relief to get these worries verbalized at long last.

Miss Franklin nodded her head and for a few moments the two women sat in companionable silence.

Repeating what parent said. "As you were talking, Mrs. Robinson, I wondered if you have been trained as a teacher because so many of your concerns about Timmy are problems commonly experienced by five-year-olds. Let's see, now you mentioned his reluctance to use the new bicycle, the occasional fights with his playmates, the dawdling, and an incident of destructiveness. These are all problems we are concerned about in working with the fives. What you said assures me that Timmy is a normal little boy who needs his mother and daddy and teacher to help in the process of growing up."

Identifying a problem. "Let's talk first about reluctance in using the bicycle," said Miss Franklin. "In school, Timmy is something of a perfectionist. I notice after block play that Timmy sorts and stacks the blocks meticulously. He is not satisfied unless they are in perfect order. He is impatient with anything he produces unless it is perfect. Often he throws away pictures which I suggest he may like to take home to you."

"Why do you think he does that?" asked Timmy's mother.

"It's too soon for me to be sure. But sometimes when parents have too high standards, a child feels that anything he does is a failure if it doesn't measure up. Of course, if a child is fearful of failure, he will be reluctant to attempt anything new."

"What you are saying is that we have had standards beyond what Timmy can do? Unless he is sure to succeed, he is afraid to try?" asked Mrs. Robinson.

"Something like that," agreed Miss Franklin. "I find myself *urging* Timmy to *try* new things. At his age level he is usually quite successful. I make it a point to emphasize his success in easel painting, finger painting, clay modelling, or whatever he tries for the first time."

"I'll tell my husband, Tim, what you have said about too high standards for Timmy. I am afraid we both have expected too much," said Mrs. Robinson.

Putting a problem into perspective. "We needn't spend too much time on the dawdling problem," laughed Miss Franklin. "It is a five-year-old characteristic that is irritating to adults but I fear we will just have to learn to live with it. The major cause of dawdling is the lack of a sense of time. Children of this age are not able to estimate the time necessary for a task, nor the passage of time while they are doing it."

"And I have gotten to be a regular nagger about it," confessed Mrs. Robinson.

Accepting feelings. "I know how you feel. Nagging actually encourages dawdling, because the child soon learns that the words mean little and that only the increasing severity of his mother's voice is a danger signal," said Miss Franklin.

"You mean I should just do nothing about it?" asked Mrs. Robinson.

Specific help. "No, not exactly. I do some things at school which you might like to try at home. A clock will help. You may make such a suggestion as, 'When the little hand gets to this point and the big hand to this point, it is time for you to be ready for school.' or 'When both hands are here, lunch will be ready.' Sometimes the child should be allowed to feel the consequences for his behavior. If he is late for school and misses some activity he was interested in, he will learn something about the importance of time. But, of course, routines give a sense of security to children. Definite times for meals, baths, and outdoor play help the child to adjust to time and anticipate his activities.

"And, we mustn't forget that children need time to experiment and enjoy their tasks. Their tasks have learning value. Tasks like lacing shoes have become commonplace to adults but are fun for children if they don't have to be completed as soon as possible."

"I can't tell you how helpful you have been. I know my time with you is about up and you have another conference. But I have worried so about the duck," began Mrs. Robinson.

Clarifying the problem. "Yes, that was really a bothersome problem," responded Miss Franklin. "Young children do not understand money values. They don't understand that it costs money to replace broken toys. I suspect, however, that Robert's duck was destroyed because of jealousy or resentment. The cure for that is for parents to assure their child of their affection. Timmy must be helped to understand that he has a secure and permanent place in his daddy's and in your affection. He is your oldest son and, much as you love Robert, no one can ever take Timmy's place in your hearts."

Mrs. Robinson looked at the clock and rose to go. "Thank you, Miss Franklin, for being so helpful with *my problems*," she said. "I am afraid I left no time to deal with yours."

Identifying with child.   "Timmy and I are still getting acquainted," answered Miss Franklin. "I have a feeling we are going to be great friends. Apparently, Timmy and I have one thing in common, we don't rush into friendships."

"I hope your friendship with Timmy can include his whole family," laughed Mrs. Robinson. "I will try to get Big Tim to come with me to our next conference."

. . . . .

Timmy's teacher felt that she had a good first conference with Timmy's mother. She had been friendly, and had tried to make Mrs. Robinson feel comfortable. She had let Mrs. Robinson get some worries off her mind. She had listened without making evaluative comments that cut off discussion. She had focused attention on Timmy, and had emphasized his strengths. She had suggested ways for Timmy's mother to try to meet her problems. Mrs. Robinson seemed to feel encouraged and said she had made a new friend.

Timmy's mother likewise felt good about her first parent conference. Timmy was his lovely teacher's "right-hand man." Bless him! How often in these difficult days with the new baby, he also had been hers, a sensitive, perceptive little boy. She felt that she had gotten some good suggestions about not holding Timmy to too high standards and about allowing time for the "dawdling," and using the clock to keep it in bounds.

"Oh," thought Mrs. Robinson, "We didn't have time to talk about the fighting. Perhaps it hasn't happened in kindergarten with the teacher right there to supervise the children all the time. Maybe that is the answer to the problem: Be on hand, and watch for danger signals."

"These parent conferences are really good," thought Mrs. Robinson. "How could I have been so afraid to go? I feel so much better about Timmy. I know he is going to have a good year in kindergarten, and we will certainly work as cooperatively as we can with his teacher. A good home and a good school are the right of every child."

Chapter Four

HANDLING
VARIOUS
CONFERENCE
SITUATIONS

In the variety of situations that arise when school people and parents evaluate the school progress of a child, or a group of children, the school person handles the conference. Often he initiates the conference, but whether he or a parent does, he needs to know how to guide the conference itself. He has studied how to work effectively with people, children or adults, and he is confident about his ability to use his conference skill in working with parents.

The usual parent depends on the school person to handle the conference, and the school person is accustomed to assuming the leadership role. However, if he is working with a parent who also has conference skill, he should be able to adapt to that situation. If the parent takes the initiative in the conference, the school person can participate in it on that basis, watching carefully to see that the conference stays on the subject and being ready to bring it back to the subject if necessary. As a participant in a conference, a school person is always responsible for seeing that the conference moves ahead smoothly. He can assume that responsibility either in the role of the leader, or in the role of another participant in the conference.

Referring a Parent

When a parent gets in touch with the school, he is apt to make the contact with whomever he feels will be understanding and sympathetic.

If he has liked a talk given by the principal, he may call the principal's office. If he feels that his child's teacher is really interested in his child, he is apt to come to the teacher. Since a parent may contact anyone at school, every school person should know how the school is organized for working effectively with parents, and should refer a parent to the person most apt to give him the assistance that he needs.

Whoever works with parents conveys or fails to convey the warmth, welcome, and friendliness of the school. No parent feels at ease if conferences are cold, indifferent or impersonal. Teachers and principals care for children and are profoundly concerned that each one does his best. The best measure of the success of a teacher or a principal is the success of the child. The spirit of concern about, and affection for, a child should be steadfastly maintained when discussing him with his parents.

The teacher works with parents whenever the child's progress in the educational program and in his classroom group is involved. The teacher is best able to provide information about the following matters, and to guide the child's subsequent progress with regard to them:

Understanding of each subject area, e.g., arithmetic, social studies

Skill in listening, speaking, reading, and writing

Ability to recognize, use, and spell words in written composition

Enjoyment of, and skill in, art, music, and other forms of aesthetic expression

Skill in contributing ideas to group discussions

Ability to follow directions, act on group decisions, and take responsibility for himself

Habits of getting to work, using time to advantage, and completing work undertaken

Feeling happy about himself and his school work

Skill in working and playing with other children constructively

Getting along with his teacher, and with other school personnel.

Since the teacher is with a child each day, she should be present whenever a conference deals with any aspects of a child's school day. The leadership that she assumes in the conference will depend on her competence as a leader in relation to the leadership competence of the other members of the conference. But whether she assumes leadership or not, she must be responsible for seeing that the conference has all pertinent information about the child's behavior and that plans for future procedures are made realistically both in terms of the child and his classroom group.

The Principal Handles Certain Conferences

The principal must work directly with a child's parents whenever the status of the child in the school is under consideration, or whenever there is the possibility of disciplinary action being necessary. Thus the principal is concerned with such problems as the following, and works with parents in arranging what is best for the child:

> *Admitting a child who is entering school for the first time, or who is transferring from another school*
> *Placing a child at the grade level at which he can work best*
> *Arranging for a child to be in the classroom of a suitable teacher*
> *Helping a child to attend school on each school day*
> *Helping a child establish good working relations with his teacher*
> *Helping a child to go to and from school safely*
> *Helping a child to play courteously and safely with other children on the playground.*

Furthermore, as the person most schooled and experienced in conference situations, the principal is the logical person to handle any conference that has reached an impasse on a controversial issue. Any conference that is difficult for a teacher to handle is usually referred to the school principal.

In schools fortunate enough to employ a counselor, the principal refers to the counselor those parent conferences requiring more time and attention than a teacher can give to an individual child and his family. The counselor thus becomes the person who works with parents when:

The teacher believes that he needs more information about a child's current or previous out-of-school behavior

Either the teacher or the parent believes that parents need more information about what the school is endeavoring to do regarding deviant behavior

The school needs to interpret classroom or playground behavior in terms of parental attitudes and values to reach a better understanding of a child

The teacher and parents are making unusually significant decisions about the future of a child

Parents feel the need to understand and evaluate the progress of their child

The teacher or principal believes that the child's progress in school is obstructed by unsocial behavior that should be studied to discover underlying causes.

The Teacher Handles a Conference

If a child has a problem involving only himself and his relationships to others in his class, his teacher helps him with his problem. In doing so, she may work with his parents. Examples of problems that a teacher in a middle-class community often can handle with a single parent conference include the following:

The young child who seems always afraid to attempt any new activity

The first or second grade child who takes money that another child has put in his desk

The child who likes to push or strike other children, and needs to learn to keep his hands to himself

The young child who engages in sex play in the classroom

The fifth or sixth grade child who imitates the dress of more sophisticated young people

The child who needs encouragement in his school work.

When a teacher first notices that a child has a problem on which he needs adult help, she should make a point of discussing it with his parents within a day or two. If she will see one of his parents at a meeting, she plans to talk with him then. If she has no opportunity for talking face to face, she can telephone. If she does not take up the problem at once, it may become more involved and in need of greater attention from the school. The following account by a school principal illustrates action which could have been obviated by earlier attention by a teacher:

The Glee Club teacher left a note saying that Gladys and Betty, two sixth-grade girls had been absent from the last two Glee Club practices, and that some of the children told her that the two girls were not coming any more because they did not like Glee Club. "Do you know anything about this?" the note asked.

I needed to find out about the Glee Club situation, but I already knew a great deal about Betty. She has never been enthusiastic about any extracurricular activity, nor about staying for any special after-school event or playground activity. Last year she became close friends with a new girl who was popular with the boys and sophisticated in both dress and manners. Much to the relief of Betty's mother, the girl moved away. This year, Betty's mother is encouraging Betty to take part in Camp Fire Girl activities, and has become assistant leader for Betty's group.

Other Camp Fire girls say that Betty is "giving her mother a bad time," and is often belligerent to her. At school the girls say that Betty is aggressive and does many underhanded things. Betty's teacher is aware of this peer attitude, as is the noon playground director. Everyone at school is working together to see if Betty can be helped to establish better values.

Gladys is a new girl who enjoys school and classroom activities. Her teacher is trying to broaden her circle of friends through work and room committees that enable the other children to become better acquainted with her.

I sent for Betty to discuss the Glee Club problem.

She said, "Mother told me to drop out."

"Why does she want you to drop out?" I asked.

"I really don't know," Betty replied.

A few minutes later she said, "Well, she wants me to help her in the mornings, and I can't get to school by 8:30."

"What do you have to do?" I asked.

Betty could not think of anything she had to do each morning other than getting breakfast and dressing for school.

I then pointed out that the notes taken home at the beginning of the school year said that it was necessary for children in Glee Club to come to school at 8:30. Her mother had signed the note indicating that she understood this and that she wanted Betty to be a member.

Betty said nothing.

"Perhaps we had better call your mother to clear up any misunderstanding," I said.

"Mother isn't home," Betty said at once. "She went to get her hair done."

"Perhaps she is back now," I said, as I dialed the number.

When Betty realized that her mother was answering the telephone, she said, "Oh, yes, I remember. It's tomorrow that she is going to have her hair done."

Betty's mother explained that Betty had been dropped from the Glee Club because she had been late. She said she thought it was unfair for the teacher to drop a girl when she had been late only once or twice.

I asked Betty's mother if she had written a note to the Glee Club teacher about the reasons for Betty's tardiness.

"No," Betty's mother said. "I did not know Betty was going to be late. The first I knew about the lateness was when Betty told me she had been kicked out of Glee Club because she was tardy."

"I am so glad to have this opportunity of talking with you," I said. "I am calling to see why you wanted Betty to drop out of the Glee Club as she said you did."

As I recounted Betty's version of the Glee Club situation, her mother was indignant. "Well, this is certainly a different story," she said.

"Have other girls been dropped from Glee Club for being late?" she asked.

"No. This has not occurred," I assured her.

"Well, I wondered about it at the time," Betty's mother said. "I thought about calling you. But I was pretty busy, and just did not find time."

I told Betty's mother that we really needed to help Betty face her problems, tell things accurately as they actually happened, and learn the consequences of being dishonest and telling falsehoods.

I talked with each of the girls separately, and then together, getting the sequence of events which resulted in the absences from Glee Club and the situation they had gotten themselves into. We talked about how one untruth usually leads to another, with no end to the lying until the whole problem is faced. Both girls contributed to the conversation and seemed to understand the situation. They agreed to talk with the Glee Club teacher to get the matter straightened out with her.

I talked with both the Glee Club teacher and the classroom teacher of the girls so that each of them can watch for situations in which to develop further ideas of facing situations honestly. We shall work with Betty's mother in any other situation that may come up, and shall get acquainted with Gladys' mother as soon as possible.

Even a situation so emotionally charged as this one can be handled pleasantly and objectively by school authorities who recognize that all children have problems as they learn to grow up and adjust to their society. Most problems are overcome by common sense attitudes on the part of parents and teachers. Teachers understand that normal children cannot be expected to behave like superior adults. If, however, a serious problem persists and parents see little improvement after efforts have been made to help the child to a more mature adjustment, then the school psychologist or psychiatrist should be consulted for further diagnosis and more specific treatment.

The Counseling Team

In a large urban elementary school, the counseling and guidance program is carried out by a team of people. Any member of the team may initiate a case study of an individual child. A teacher observing a child in the classroom will be most apt to be the first person to sense that the child's world is in need of more adult guidance than it is receiving. However, a parent may observe the child at home and in other out-of-school situations, and may seek assistance from the school by discussing the child's behavior with any one of the counseling team.

As soon as a case is initiated, the counseling team moves into action, each specialist making his contribution as the team works to smooth the way of the child. As the case proceeds, a member of the counseling team may be absent from school, with a substitute taking over his responsibilities for a few days.

The necessity for effective team work implies that communication among members of the team must be excellent. Each member must know what to observe about the child; how to work with the child; and what to discuss with the parents. This interaction of school personnel with parents is illustrated in the case report described. A more simple case involves fewer members of the school staff. Yet any case study should reveal relevant information from all sources. The team work as well as the kind of situation described in the following report could have occurred in any urban elementary school:

CASE STUDY OF GARY GOODWIN

Early in January

The mother of Gary Goodwin, a pupil in second grade, called the school and talked with the principal about whether or not it would be advisable for her son to go back into the first grade. As they talked, the principal made notes on sheets of paper to discuss with the teacher and counselor:

> *Gary is out of school ill.*
> *Mother thinks he may need to go back into first grade.*
> *Gary feels that other children in the second grade do not want to play with him.*
> *Gary is quite small for his age.*
> *His asthma may be brought on by pressure of school tasks and unhappiness in his relations with his playmates.*

In referring the case to the counselor, the principal wrote the following suggestions:

> *Take a look at the child and talk with Gary's teacher.*
> *See what you and the teacher think about grade placement and relations with other children.*

I told Gary's mother that we would call her back next week.

Ten Days Later

The counselor had made notes about Gary's classroom behavior as a basis for talking with Gary's mother. The notes were as follows:

> *Gary is on the fringe of the classroom group.*
> *Gary often needs attention. He demands praise for each small accomplishment.*
> *His work is not consistent.*
> *He is reading in primers.*
> *He has difficulty with arithmetic and with spelling.*
> *He told his teacher that his mother never looks at the papers he takes home and that she does not talk with him about what happens in school.*

The counselor called Gary's mother at work:
"Hello, Mrs. Goodwin?"
"Hello. This is Mrs. Goodwin."

"Mrs. Goodwin, this is the counselor at Gary's school. Is this a good time to talk about Gary, or would you rather call me back?"

As the conversation continued, the counselor made notes about Mrs. Goodwin's comments, and about her suggestions, as follows:

Gary often blinks.

Gary was hospitalized when he was a preschool boy. He felt deserted. Since then he often has a tantrum about being left alone.

Counselor suggests praise of what Gary does, looking at magazines together, talking about what they see on a walk.

Counselor will give tests to see where Gary needs help, and will talk with him each week.

Mother and counselor will keep in touch as they see how Gary develops.

Later in the Month

The counselor talked with Gary after he had been absent one day:

"Who was with you at home?" the counselor asked.

"Nobody," Gary replied.

"Were you pretty sick?" the counselor asked.

"I took pills," Gary said.

"When did you take the pills?" the counselor asked.

"Mother called me from work," Gary explained.

The counselor was concerned about a second-grade boy being at home by himself when he was ill. When the matter was discussed with the school nurse, she said that Gary had an attendance problem. He would be in school for a day, then out for a day.

When Gary was again absent a few days later, the school nurse reported the absence to the supervisor of child welfare and attendance. He made a home visit and found Gary at home by himself. He then called Mrs. Goodwin at work. She said that in a few days she would come to discuss the matter.

The First of February

Mrs. Goodwin came to the school office to request that Gary repeat the first grade. She said that Gary uses his asthmatic illness as an excuse for staying home.

The next day Gary's new first-grade teacher welcomed Gary as warmly as had his second-grade teacher. Gary has good rapport with teachers and counselors as well as his playmates.

The Latter Part of March

Gary's teacher reported that Gary was absent, and that his attendance pattern seemed to be one day at school followed by three days out of school. The counselor telephoned Gary's home. His mother said that Gary was ill with an upset stomach, laryngitis, and diarrhea. He had fallen off his bicycle the day before and was seeing double.

"Have you called the doctor?" inquired the counselor.

"No, I haven't. I'm getting very anxious about Gary because I have to go back to work soon."

Mrs. Goodwin talked on while the counselor took notes in the form of quotes:

"I'm never sure whether he is sick or not. The nurse sent him home from school one day with a fever."

"His father resents not being able to cope with him. Sometimes he gets furious and spanks him. Do you think he should do that?"

"Mostly his father closes his mind to what Gary does."

"We were separated for about a year when Gary was little."

"I can't stand to send him off to school when he's ill. I have to cope with my own feelings, too."

A Few Days Later

Mrs. Goodwin brought Gary to school about an hour late. After he had been admitted, the counselor took Gary to his room. Mrs. Goodwin accompanied them.

"You go on in now," Mrs. Goodwin said to Gary, hesitantly.

"You wait in the car for me," Gary demanded.

"But I have some things to do at home," Mrs. Goodwin said lamely.

"Goodbye, Mrs. Goodwin," said the counselor firmly. "Gary will be home after school."

The Following Monday Morning

After discussing the case with the social worker on the staff, the counselor called Mrs. Goodwin:

"Mrs. Goodwin, we are fortunate in having a special counselor available occasionally. He is coming to our school this afternoon, and I have asked him to save some time for you. Can you come?"

"Oh, I'd like to come. Can my husband come too? I'll try to talk him into it," Mrs. Goodwin said as she made arrangements for a conference at 3:15.

At one o'clock Mrs. Goodwin telephoned the counselor to say

that Gary was seeing double, that she had called the doctor, and that she had to take Gary to the doctor at two o'clock.

"I can't come at three o'clock," she said, "but I'll leave a note for my husband to come."

At three o'clock Gary's well-dressed father had a conference with the social worker. The social worker made notes as follows:

So far as Mr. Goodwin is concerned, Gary will be at school every day from now on.

Gary's father mentioned much parental strife.

Referred father to Family Service for counseling as needed.

In April

Mrs. Goodwin attended the Open House evening when every teacher received parents who came to visit.

"Gary has been coming every day," his teacher said. "We are so glad, too, that he has been doing much better in his school work these past two weeks."

"That's very interesting," Mrs. Goodwin replied. "His father and I have been separated for two weeks."

In this case, as is true in many others, the causes of Gary's behavior were multiple, complex, and interrelated. To a physical condition of low vitality was added fear generated by a frightening early illness in which Gary developed feelings of anxiety about being deserted.

His out-of-school life reveals none of the qualities of a calm, harmonious, supportive environment essential to the optimum development of a mature human being. Marital discord was the rule rather than the exception. Recurrent separations and reconciliations of parents intensified the inescapable feelings of insecurity that occupied the center of Gary's existence. He actually had no life space in which he could expect consistent affection or discipline. When family counseling was recommended, Gary's father and mother evidently did not take advantage of this opportunity to explore the effect of their lack of parental responsibility, and were so egocentric and irresponsible that they were more concerned with their personal gratifications than with their son's needs.

Elements in such a situation make the problem beyond solution for school people regardless of their awareness of the damage to the child's personality. However, this awareness does make it possible to intervene in behalf of the child in significant ways. Demonstration of the interest and affection the child must have for normal development can be supplied by a generous, understanding teacher. Vital experiences in the curriculum can develop motivation and attitudes essential to the child's maturation. Somehow, when teachers know a great deal about a child, they seem to find the means to compensate, at least partially, for deficiencies in the child's out-of-school environment.

Drawing Lines of Responsibility

In working with parents, school people must have in their minds a clear map about the responsibility that parents take for their children, and the responsibility that the school takes. Parents and school need to draw on that map a definite boundary line, with a defined area in which parents and school share responsibility. The line is not hard and fast. Betty's mother, for instance, who was a more responsible mother in a disadvantaged school community, readily shared responsibility with the school to meet Betty's needs. Gary's parents, at the time that Gary needed more adult help, were not only less responsible than they usually were, but also less responsible than others in their school community. A hard and fast expectation of what parents should do could have kept the school from meeting these children's needs adequately.

Depending upon the social groups that constitute the school community, the line of responsibility may be drawn one way in one school and somewhat differently in the next school. A school person who moves to a new school district comes to know where the line of responsibility is drawn in the school, and the respects in which the line differs from the line he knew in his previous school. Also, when the community around an urban school gradually reflects a shift in the social groups that populate the area, the school people find themselves drawing a new line of responsibility.

In one community a sudden change occurred when a base was established by the government for training air force cadets. With the influx of the families of commanding officers, the school found that it had added families who were vitally concerned with the kind of experiences their children had. The newly arrived parents valued experiences that were a part of the school program, but they also valued travel. The requests of parents that their children be excused from school for several days or even a week at a time became more numerous. The school found itself faced with considering, for instance, how valuable it is for children to be absent from school in order to:

- *Have orthodontic treatment from an outstanding specialist in a nearby city*
- *Accompany mother on a shopping expedition in the city*
- *Accompany father on a hunting trip in another part of the country*
- *Accompany the family on a trip to the private school attended by an older brother or sister*
- *Take part in a family vacation trip to another nation*
- *See national parks in the United States.*

Should the school set up a policy based on the fact that average daily attendance is the basis for school support by state funds? Or should it attempt to assay the educational values for the child in each individual parent request? Or should it assume that an absence requested by a parent was *ipso facto* a request to be granted? These were questions which school board members, school administrators, teachers, and other school personnel have to be able to answer in working with parents. Furthermore, to maintain the confidence of the community in the school, school people have to be consistent in their responses to such questions.

A school in the center of a metropolitan area had entirely different requests from the parents of its children. For instance, when the seventh-grade rooms centered their studies on plans for a week of camping in the nearby mountains, notes went home to the parents advising them about what each child would need in coping with a climate colder than he had experienced, and pointing out that the extraordinary expenses of the week were to be met by the payment of ten dollars per child. A week or two later a conscientious mother receiving welfare assistance came in to ask about filling out forms so that her oldest daughter could go on the trip with her expenses taken care of. She was shocked to learn that educational agencies differ from welfare ones. With the help of the principal, her daughter was able in the next months to earn the money by working regularly after school for an hour in the office of the school nurse.

To bridge the gap between parent responsibility and school responsibility in such communities, school personnel consider what plans of action are in keeping with their educational objectives. Should there be a PTA fund from which pupils without lunch money can borrow if they need to and if they have repaid previous loans? Should the budget include a fund for girls or boys needing to earn money for special school events or activities outside of school? Should "deserving" children be identified as recipients of scholarships provided by families of higher income? These are the kinds of questions that school personnel in some communities must answer in arriving at school policy in working with parents and their children. The kinds of activities initiated and continued by the school, and the kind and amount of guidance provided by the school, are important parts of school policy.

In the school in the middle-class community, drawing the line of responsibility between parents and school involves a minimum of problems because of general agreement regarding the school goals and values, and the practices of parents concerning what should be done for the children. However, particularly in the urban school, there are apt to be two or three families whose circumstances differ from those of the community as a whole, and whose level of responsibility differs from the usual expectation level. How the school works with such a family is illustrated in the following report about Lorna:

Comments by Fourth Grade Teacher

November: Lorna brought a can of frozen soup for the needy family.

January: Lorna was an hour late to school because her only pair of shoes were in the drier.

February: Lorna refused to talk about the pre-teen parties she attends at the Recreation Center. I called the mothers of each of the three girls involved in these parties. Lorna's mother, like the others, feels it is nice that her daughter is popular.

March: Lorna and the other two "party" girls, together with a fourth girl, left school at noon to have lunch at a nearby drive-in. One of their mothers happened to see the girls and brought them back to school without informing either the teacher or principal of the incident. The fourth girl was so upset that she tearfully confessed what had happened.

When the principal called each of the parents and informed them about the rules preventing students from leaving school without permission, Lorna's mother remarked that the girls were rather clever to think of going to the drive-in, and that "girls will be girls."

April: Lorna's mother stopped in after school. She says she is concerned about Lorna's "boy friend." He often telephones when it is nine o'clock and Lorna is in bed. Lorna became quite upset when her mother refused to let her speak with him.

It was not clear whether Lorna's mother was worried about Lorna having a "boy friend" at an earlier age than her two older sisters did, or wanted to confide in someone about Lorna's skill in gaining such attention. At any rate, this is the first indication that the mother is concerned about Lorna's behavior.

Lorna was not in school here for the fifth grade, but returned to the school district for the sixth grade.

Comment by Principal

This fall Lorna has been reported several times as one of the girls congregating in the lavatory to comb, brush, rearrange, and then spray their fancy hair-dos during the recess period. The girls were called into the office to discuss their use of the recess period. It was explained that both at school and work, people are expected to enjoy physical activity as a change from concentration and work. It was also pointed out that a hair arrangement for school or employment should be one requiring no attention. A hair arrangement should not distract either its wearer or its audience. For these reasons, the school has a rule that hair spray is not to be brought to school.

Comment by Counselor

Lorna is often in my office to ask for a safety pin to keep a strap from falling down over her arm, to repair a ripped armhole seam or to repair a hem or waistline seam temporarily.

Any morning at nine o'clock I am apt to have Lorna come to say, "My mother told me to come and get a new band-aid." One morning bandages were needed over her entire leg. Her first attempt to shave her legs had resulted in deep and jagged cuts.

Comments by Sixth-Grade Teacher

Lorna has seemed more subdued the latter part of this year. The hair spray problem occurred early in the year as did another attempt to have lunch outside school. Lorna went home one noon with another socially mature sixth-grade girl who is a year older. The girls are no longer speaking to each other.

Popular girls in class do not include Lorna in their peer group. She is on the fringe, together with another girl of similar social status. Apparently she is making fewer attempts to gain recognition through questionable actions.

The files about Lorna are much like any other school files for upper-grade girls who are early in their physiological maturation or in their eagerness to take on ways they admire in older girls. But school files vary in the parent attitudes that they report. A middle-class mother is interested in her daughter remaining a child who enjoys childish pleasures. She thinks ahead to vocational preparation or college, and tries to prevent emotional involvements which might interfere with that goal. But mothers in other social groups have different views. Some abrogate their responsibility for guiding their children as soon as possible. Others are eager to guide their daughters into early marriage, sometimes to gain social status for themselves through this achievement, and sometimes to have their daughters achieve the kind of family life they value for themselves.

The school needs to know what proportion of its families are identified with each of such views. It also needs to decide the extent to which it will help each group of parents in upholding their views and teaching them to their children. Should the school leave to family education the matter of the age level at which to marry? Should the school prepare the children to look forward to college if only a small percentage of them can be expected to complete it? Each school must answer such questions in determining its parent policies.

The faculty of every school should develop policies regarding the social behavior of its pupils, including those who are more mature, and should consistently put them into effect in its conferences with parents. These policies may coincide with the practices and beliefs that the teachers have had in effect in their own lives, or they may be different from them.

Decisions as to policy should be made on the basis of recognizing objectively the needs and interests of the pupils, and developing means for helping them become members of the community who are able to earn a living and look after themselves. A faculty must be realistic about the amount of responsibility that pupils will be able to take as adults. It should have ambitions for the pupils in keeping with their talents and with the times.

Currently, girls should be prepared for responsibility in the home and outside it. Since one-third of the working force is now feminine, and a girl can expect to be employed outside the home for twenty-five years during her lifetime, she should look forward to marriage *and* a career. Similarly, boys should look forward to having jobs and families. Both girls and boys need to appreciate that the day of the strong arm and back has been followed by the day of the machine tended by the man or woman of any creed or color who is able to read and follow directions. Parents and school must work together in preparing girls and boys for the lives they will lead.

Chapter Five

THE CHALLENGE OF
WORKING WITH
SOCIOECONOMICALLY
DISADVANTAGED
PARENTS_____

Working with parents in socioeconomically disadvantaged families is a major challenge to the elementary schools of the United States. When President Lyndon B. Johnson focused nationwide attention on families with lower incomes, he opened a new frontier not only for the expanding economy but also for education.

Children of rich and poor alike attend elementary schools. Their parents and the schools have the responsibility for preparing all of the children for their places in the social order. But the limitations of the socioeconomically disadvantaged parents make the schools the major agent in preparing their children to earn a living and assume the responsibilities of citizenship. If the teacher is to guide effectively the learning of such children, then he needs to understand the nature and problems of the less advantaged families and the ways in which both he and the principal of his school work with them.

Who Are the Socioeconomically Disadvantaged?

In general the socioeconomically disadvantaged families are those who find it difficult to provide for themselves and their children. They deviate in one or more respects from the stereotype envisioned as the Average American Family: a father who has skills needed and rewarded by the American economy; a mother who has not only the skills which make her a good wife and mother but also those which enable her to find a place in the economy during periods of pressure on the financial structure of the family; children who are growing up as good members of the family and of the school.

Usually the fragmented family is a socioeconomically disadvantaged one. If the father takes responsibility for one or two children, he has difficulty in earning the money needed for his little family unit and in being available to the children during the hours that they are not in school. If the mother is the head of a family, she may find it even more difficult to be wage-earner and parent. Usually she earns less than a man earns, as is shown in the table on page 85. If she has only domestic skills, the social order rewards her efforts with low wages. Providing the necessities of life for herself and her children is not easy. The children of such fragmented families reflect the limitations of the environments their parents can provide.

The newly arrived and the nonwhite family are more apt to be among the socioeconomically disadvantaged families than is the white family. Caucasians constitute the bulk of the American society, and they tend to shut out families that are different. Immigrant families must learn to speak the language of their new country and to act as its present residents do. The new families enter the social order at a low level and rise through its social groups on the basis of their skills. Those whose skin color differs from that of the Caucasian also must perfect their skills to a high level to gain entrance to, and hold, jobs that pay well enough to provide socioeconomic advantages for their families. The social pressures on such families are felt by their children.

Socioeconomically disadvantaged families include those whose wage earners are classified in the unskilled labor occupations. These workers are rapidly being displaced by machines. Those who remain are often mobile or migratory. They take their children out of school to rush after phantom jobs rumored in connection with recently awarded government contracts, as well as to follow the seasonal harvesting of crops. Neither the fragmentary schooling, the insecurity of family income nor the accompanying health hazards are to the advantage of the children.

The socioeconomically disadvantaged families are in the limelight of the poverty program because they are among the 47 million families who in 1962 had incomes below $3,000. They are described[1] as including about half of the Indian and Negro families, about one-third of the Puerto Rican and Mexican families, and somewhat less than one-fifth of

INCOME OF FAMILIES[1]	
Family Description	*Median Income*
Male Head	$7,803
Female Head	4,010
White	7,722
Non-white	4,628

[1] Bureau of Census, U.S. Department of Commerce, "Consumer Income," Series P-60, No. 53 (December 28, 1967), pages 23, 24.

the white families of the United States. As a group, these poor include:

11 million children
Fatherless families
Farm and non-farm families, as well as urban ones
Half of the families headed by someone over age 65
Adults with less than eighth-grade education
Workers displaced by technological change.

Furthermore, they reproduce themselves. Poverty "is handed down from generation to generation in a cycle of inadequate education, inadequate homes, inadequate jobs, and stunted ambitions."[2]

Teachers who work with children from socioeconomically disadvantaged families come to know the families on the basis of how they reinforce the school. Certain phrases in the conversation of school personnel reflect anticipation of potential problems at school. These include:

[1] Catherine Chilman and Marvin B. Sussman, "Poverty in the United States in the Mid-Sixties," *Journal of Marriage and the Family* (November, 1964), pages 391–5.
[2] "The War on Poverty: The Economic Opportunity Act of 1964," materials prepared for the Select Subcommittee on Poverty of the Committee on Labor and Public Welfare, United States Senate. Washington, D.C. Pages 35–36.

The father supports the family by doing odd jobs, sometimes available locally, sometimes available out-of-town, and sometimes not available (with concomitant emotional and migration problems in the life of the family, actually or potentially interfering with pupil accomplishment at school).

The child probably has a common-law family (which does not value or teach certain social customs considered important by school personnel).

There is no father in the family (to provide money for school lunch and other school expenses, medical and dental care).

The family speaks its native language at home (rather than the English taught at school).

In a middle-class community, a child is surrounded by examples of people who have achieved lives that are happy, worthwhile, and attractive. He sees his family able to provide food and clothing for its children. He has as much as many others, and more than "the poor." But in the socioeconomically disadvantaged community, the reality of the present and the prospect of the future are not always attractive. The following account of the discouraging life of a fourth-grade boy can be duplicated with variations in any school serving a disadvantaged neighborhood. Sympathetic, understanding school people are needed who take time to listen to and to encourage both children and parents in developing self-confidence.

Kenneth has attended our school for several years and has been a behavior problem all of that time. Ken originally lived with his mother and several siblings, but at the present time the mother and father are separated, and Ken lives with the father. However, the mother lives in the same apartment house, cooks Ken's breakfast, and gets him off to school in the morning, although she is remarried and is now Mrs. Brown. Both the mother and father appear to be in poor health. They are unkempt when they come to school, and are not clean. The father, especially, is dirty.

The father, who has only one arm, has come to school at various times during the day. He is a caretaker at a theater and works at night after the movie is over. On occasion, Ken has gone with him to clean and has stayed all night working in the theater.

At a conference last year, Mrs. Brown indicated that when the baby was about to be born just three years ago, she felt that she could not take care of all of her children, so she gave a three-year-old daughter out for adoption. Ken and this girl were very close. The mother felt that Ken resented her doing this.

In talking to Ken, it becomes evident that he cares little for his mother. His mother seems to reject him also. One of Ken's friends said at one time that Ken mentioned that he would like to have a mother.

Today in talking to Ken, I asked what his father had said about his being truant the other day. He said that nothing was said. Then finally he said, "My father beat me with my shoe."

So I asked him, "Was it a bad spanking? Does this mean that you won't do it again?"

He said, "I will do it again if I get mad enough."

He went ahead to say, "I imagine I will end up in the penitentiary when I am about nineteen."

I asked him, "What makes you think this?"

He said, "Well, everybody tells me that."

"What do you mean by everybody?" I asked.

He said, "My mother."

"What other fears does she have?" I asked, leading him into a discussion about fears, the fact that everyone has some fears, and the need for us not to be influenced by the fears of others.

"I think you will end up looking after yourself when you are nineteen; perhaps looking after others as well," I said as he left the school.

A Way Out of the Poverty Spiral

Escape from the poverty spiral, educators feel, can be facilitated by providing information about opportunities available to those who seek them out, and motivation for leaving familiar surroundings and venturing out to take advantage of those opportunities. One of the people who has demonstrated what can be done by working with parents in scoioeconomically disadvantaged communities is Dr. Samuel Shepard, Jr., Assistant Superintendent of the Banneker School District in St. Louis.[3] Through home visits and parent meetings, as well as in the classroom, teachers of his district get across to the Negro families that schooling is the preventive to being out of work and the means for earning the pay that any other school graduate earns. Negro speakers testify that they have salaries and offers of other positions on the basis of their skills.

[3] Paul Friggens, "Is the Negro Equal in Intelligence and Ability?" *The Reader's Digest* (March, 1964). Pages 83–87.

Parents obtain discarded dictionaries and other books for their children. They sign a Pledge of Cooperation with the school and turn off the TV and radio so that the children can study. They get their children to school on time and with homework papers completed. The result is not only a drop in school vandalism, improved attendance at school, but also greater ability to master the tasks of the school.

Working with Every Parent

The school must help each child develop the talents that he has to the point where he can become so useful to the society that he will earn an adequate income in adult life. In working with each child, the school must also work with his parents. In doing this, the school must recognize that every person has a place in our society, that a socioeconomically disadvantaged family is not necessarily of inadequate ability, and that the cooperation of parents can speed up the time it takes a child to learn and can enrich his learning. Whatever parents can do to help their children is to be encouraged by the school.

Theoretically, it is possible for the school to work with every parent for the good of his child or children. In actual practice, however, a few men and women who have the title of "parent" are not willing or able to assume the responsibility that goes with it. For instance, the lone parent who is a confirmed alcoholic is not apt to be an effective parent. Social agencies may spend years helping him with his personal problems before he will be able to function adequately as a parent. Meanwhile, the school may better spend time and energy in working directly with the child and the family social worker.

When a school person talks with a child about his responsibility, the child may threaten, "I won't do it, and you can't make me. I'll call my social worker!" In such a situation, the school calls the social agency and works with it as well as with the parents for the good of the child.

Often the family that is most difficult for the school to work with is the family that is most in need of help—but not necessarily from the school. The school must be able to differentiate between what it can do for such families and what must be done by other social agencies. As Dr. Cummings points out:

> The school cannot rebuild the slums . . . The schools over a long period of time may improve human relations by mitigating prej-

udice, but other community agencies have an equal responsibility in changing community attitudes. The schools cannot provide adequate medical and psychiatric services or social services for deprived families. It cannot enforce the laws which are designed to provide a moral climate favorable for civic living. These are tasks for the whole community.[4]

Contrasts with Middle Class

The educator working with socioeconomically disadvantaged parents needs to understand their ways in contrast to the ways that he knows. The school man is a member of the middle class. As such he unconsciously behaves in certain ways. He approves behavior like his own, and he tends to reject behavior that is different from his.

However, being aware of this tendency and of the differences between middle-class behavior and the behavior of socioeconomically disadvantaged people, he can learn how to work with parents who are socioeconomically disadvantaged.

Socioeconomically disadvantaged families are apt to differ from middle-class ones in several of the following respects:

Socioeconomically Disadvantaged Families	*Middle Class Families*
1. Are disinterested or negative about schooling	1. Are interested in schooling
2. Are apathetic about, or opposed to, what the school does	2. Back the school in what it does
3. Expect their children will not use their schooling	3. Expect their children to profit from schooling
4. Do not have money for school activities, even school lunch in some instances	4. Willing and able to pay costs of schooling and of medical and dental care
5. Include a high number of mobile and migratory families	5. Include a high proportion of stable families
6. Have difficulty in providing a suitable study situation	6. Able and willing to provide a quiet study situation for children

[4] Howard H. Cummings, "Conclusions," *Programs for the Educationally Disadvantaged*. Washington, D.C.: U.S. Government Printing Office, 1963. Page 105.

Socioeconomically Disadvantaged	*Families* *Middle Class Families*
7. Do not have educational materials at home	7. Provide educational materials at home, e.g., educational television, reference books, newspapers, and magazines
8. Primarily are interested in meeting their individual needs	8. Greatly interested in meeting the needs of their own and other children
9. Do not point out educational aspects of experience	9. Provide educational experiences, e.g., trips, camping, music lessons, family activities, Scout and other group activities
10. Are not apt to recall school-related memories favorably	10. Able to interpret what children see accurately and favorably
11. Set an example of opposition to or non-compliance with authority	11. Recognize authority and teach children to recognize it
12. Tackle problems with physical fighting and grudges	12. Tackle problems with verbal exchange, and any problem-solving techniques they have learned
13. Do not anticipate a secure future	13. Look forward to an attractive future through work

The middle-class teacher entering a school in a disadvantaged community can either suffer cultural shock, or can try to understand how other people have solved their problems of surviving in a community that has limited resources. His interest in, and appreciation of, culturally disadvantaged people[5] can create a setting favorable for his ways to be appreciated and tried out by the people he serves.

For a school person, going from the middle-class neighborhood where he lives into a school neighborhood of contrasting characteristics is much like going into a foreign land. Like the traveler, the school man can encapsulate himself within his own culture and look at the customs of the foreigners as less desirable than his. Or, like the wise traveler, he can try to understand how people in a different set of circumstances have

[5] Frank Riessman, *The Culturally Deprived Child.* New York: Harper & Row, Publishers, 1962.

worked out solutions to the problems of providing their families with the necessities and niceties of life. His interest in their way of life endears him to newly found friends, and he lays a basis for some of his ways of living and thinking to rub off and be assimilated into theirs.

Both the educator and the traveler find certain aspects of behavior more important to consider than other aspects. "Are these people friendly and eager to learn?" is a more practical question than, "What kind of costumes do these people wear?" or "What table manners have they developed?" The educator working with socioeconomically disadvantaged families has a great deal to do to help them in preparing their children to earn a living. He needs to keep his attention focused on teaching the most essential knowledge and skills, ignoring for the time being costumes and social customs that are not critical factors in the life of the child at his age level. A good time for teaching the child about them is when they become matters of concern to him. But to try to teach them at the same time that many basic skills are to be taught may be so overwhelming as to interfere with learning the basic skills. The wise school person develops judgment about what to teach at any given time.

Getting Parent Backing for the School

The disadvantaged parent is silent or even resentful and disparaging about the school. The middle-class parent, on the other hand, tells his child, "You have to learn to get along with all kinds of people. You had better learn how to work with your teacher because the world has many such people in it." Thus the second parent helps his child solve the problem of establishing a relationship with his teacher, but the first parent does not.

If a satisfactory child-teacher relationship is to be developed, the school has to give time and attention to the problem. In working with socioeconomically disadvantaged families, school personnel cannot assume that parents are reinforcing what the school is trying to teach them. The teachers, counselors, and principals who listen to what children say soon accumulate comments to the contrary, comments that reveal what parents say at home about school.

In one school, for instance, a series of incidents all showed the same parental view about Don's teacher. When Don was talking with the school principal, he said that he did not like his teacher and did not like her "yelling at him" and trying to make him work. He also said that his father had called her an "old lady" and said that she was too old to be teaching a class.

A few days later, his teacher sent Don to the office with the following note:

> When I went to the playground to get my class, Don and his friend Ray were screaming, "Old lady, old lady!"
>
> Yesterday when I asked Don in a nice way to remain in the seat to which I had had to move him, he said, "I wish you were dead."

When Don was taking some tests with the counselor, he told her that his father had said his teacher was an old lady, too old to teach.

To help Don relate to his teacher better, the principal arranged a parent conference which attempted to gain parental cooperation. Here is the principal's report on the conference:

> The conference with Mr. Swanson turned out to be very satisfactory. What I tried to get across to Don's father was that the only thing that was going to make any difference in his son's progress in school was whether his father would play on our team and support the teacher and the school. I kept making this point to the father—that he was the one that had to do it, that he had to support the school and the program, not passively, but actively. I did not want him just not to say anything against the school—as I am sure he has—but to say positive things and build up the school and the teacher. He has to let his son know that he's working with the school.
>
> I told Mr. Swanson that he has a fine boy. Don is smart. He is nice looking, healthy, and a good athlete.
>
> After our conference, Mr. Swanson said he would try to do this. I then talked both to Don and his father as we walked out of the office. I said to Don, "Your father and I have had a nice talk. He and I are good friends, and we're going to work at things the same way. We are going to understand one another and understand how to help you. Your father is a friend of the school. He likes our school, and he wants you to get something out of it." I said this in front of Don in order to commit Mr. Swanson to this course of action. This conference shows some promise, if the father can follow through.

Don's teacher, Miss Smith, also realized that Don had a problem which was interfering with his accomplishment of school tasks. His problem, she reasoned, is apt to be one that other children have in this kind of community. Someone like Don's father probably wonders how long he can hold his job, and looks at other people in terms of this question. When she was planning social studies work for the following week, Miss Smith saw how a discussion would fit in on the topic, "Do fathers work all their lives?"

When she had a few minutes alone with Don, Miss Smith previewed the class discussion. She told him about social security—how a worker's earnings not only give him money to live on now but also later, when he no longer works. She told him, too, that the boss decides how long a father is able to work on his job, and that the school board decides how long teachers should teach.

The counselor in the school also helped with Don's problem. She knew that "name calling" is a continuing problem to children in the upper grades and to the people who work with them.

She arranged for name calling to be the topic of discussion at the next teachers' meeting so that all teachers would be working together to reduce or eliminate it. She watched for individual cases of name calling in which she could help the children to learn how best to cope with the problem.

In much the same way, she brought to the teachers the continuing problems that children have in adjusting to financial difficulties at home.

Name calling or any other bid for attention can be evidence that a child is encountering problems on which he needs help. The school should try to diagnose the child's need and assist him with his basic problem as well as with his symptomatic ones.

Recognizing Boundaries of Authority

The following example further illustrates how school people work with the parents as well as the children. The community must understand that the school has its way of working, and that this may be different from the ways now in use in the homes and in the neighborhood. Here is a brief report about how a school and one of its families are working toward a mutual understanding about where the boundaries of authority lie, and how the rules of behavior differ within each set of boundaries. Of course, the school is realistic about having to teach each year what the boundaries and appropriate behaviors are.

The Sabola boys have been in the office frequently during the past three years for threatening to hit someone after school. When talked with, their answer has always been that their father told them not to let anyone pick on them, and that whatever their father told them to do they always did. The father has been invited into the school. Each time he comes we have tried to help him see that the school has many adults who can help the children work out a problem peacefully instead of fighting. Mr. Sabola has agreed that he will let us do this whenever any incident happens at school, but at home, after school hours and on the weekend, he feels that the boys must protect themselves.

After one incident early in the school year there has been no other problem with either of the boys so far as the playground or the school is concerned. Furthermore, the father has written a note saying that he will give us full cooperation at school but that he does not feel that we should engage, or be interested, in what happens on the way home from school. With this point of view the school authorities are unable to concur.

When we saw the father at Open House, we thanked him for his note and his excellent cooperation. We pointed out, however, that both parents and school people are concerned that children go safely and happily between home and school and that both are legally responsible for children's behavior at such times.

Guiding Parents in Helping Their Children

Currently it is recognized that parents in the socioeconomically disadvantaged communities make limited use of desirable methods of helping their children. Parents in middle-class communities, on the other hand, often include teachers and others who know and use effective methods for guiding their children. This parental difference is brought out in a study by Robert D. Hess at the University of Chicago. He observed and analyzed the interaction of mothers with their four-year-old children in certain task situations. He describes reactions of middle-class and then socioeconomically disadvantaged mothers to one of the task situations as follows:[6]

> The task of the mother is to teach the child how to group or sort a small number of toys . . .
> The first mother . . . outlines the task for the child, giving sufficient help and explanation to permit the child to proceed alone . . .

[6] Robert D. Hess, "Educability and Rehabilitation: The Future of the Welfare Class," *Journal of Marriage and the Family* (November, 1964), pages 422–29.

> This mother . . . offered support and help of various kinds;
> and . . . impelled the child to perform. . . .

In contrast to the helpful explanation and supportive guidance of the
middle-class mother is the nonverbal communication of another mother
who does not provide her child

> . . . with the essential information he needs to solve or to under-
> stand the problem. There is clearly some impelling on the part
> of the mother for the child to perform, but the child has not been
> told what he is to do.

Commenting on this second kind of interaction, Dr. Hess points out
that:

> The consequence of this sort of exchange affects both the cogni-
> tive ability of the child (in that he is not taught how to deal
> with problems) and also his motivation for achievement and sense
> of self-confidence because the experience is essentially frustrating.

The contrast between parental support and guidance that Dr. Hess
found at the preschool level exists throughout the elementary school.
The middle-class mother is ready with a realistic explanation when it is
needed. For instance, she pictures the school as a place to learn, and
teachers as people who are like parents in helping children. But the
mother from the socioeconomically disadvantaged area is not ready with a
verbal explanation. Instead, if she is present when her child has a question
to ask, she is apt to be uninformed or to make some brief, status-oriented
reply. For her child, she builds the concept of school as a place where
"you have to be good, and do what the teacher says."

The parent from the socioeconomically disadvantaged community
knows one means of guidance for his children: spanking. If the child
gets into difficulty, his parent spanks him. When a child has problems
at school his parent advises the school to spank him.

The following account of a series of parent conferences shows how
the principal of a school attempted to help a mother cope with her
problems and those of her child on a more understanding basis. Encouraging parents and suggesting ways in which they can encourage their
children is an important part of work with parents. It benefits both the
child in school and the children who will come later.

Bobby Schmidt is a pupil in the first grade this year and is also enrolled in our child-care program which extends his care through the working day. Bobby was a problem in kindergarten last year, and the child-care nursery school teacher has also commented on the fact that he is difficult to handle.

After the first two weeks of school, Bobby's first-grade teacher related some of his adjustment problems. Bobby pinches and hits people. On one occasion he stuck some children with pins. He gets very angry on the playground. He finds it hard to do his work, although his teacher says that he has the ability to do it if he would apply himself.

Today I had a third conference with Mrs. Schmidt. She is separated, possibly divorced, from her husband and lives alone with Bobby. She is going to school to become a beauty operator. She is an extremely tense woman, probably under considerable pressure. She has a serious look on her face although she is an attractive young woman. She never smiles. She sees the negative side of every topic of conversation. She feels that Bobby is not a good boy and that she is not a good parent. After running herself down as a parent, she then defends herself and says that she is doing the best she can.

When I informed Mrs. Schmidt that Bobby does not show good self-control with the teacher and with the other boys and girls in the classroom, she replied that she spanks him frequently and that this is the best she can do. I pointed out that, although he may respond to her treatment at home, he is not responding at school. When I asked her whether she thought we should use the same spanking technique that she uses, she said that she would not favor the idea. Therefore I told her, "All right. I won't paddle him." I said that when he was beyond our control, we would call her and she would have to do something about her boy.

This year, Bobby's teacher reported that he was having difficulties again. Two weeks after school started, I called his mother in for conferences with Bobby's teacher and me.

Mrs. Schmidt was again nervous and pale. She fiddled with her purse and with her keys. She continued to make derogatory remarks about herself and her youngster. After listening to this for a while, I decided to talk to her about herself rather than about Bobby. I suggested that the burden of being Bobby's only support was causing her much anxiety, and that when she completed her schooling and got a job, she would feel better. She said that she did not see it this way. She was under unbearable pressure and would continue to be under it. I pointed out that many people have difficult times during their lives when they think they cannot see daylight, but that it usually clears up and, with perseverance and some faith, this would clear up, too, and she would be under less pressure.

I suggested to Mrs. Schmidt that she was a tense and nervous person, and she agreed to this. I then talked in terms of how she could show Bobby more affection and take a positive approach to his problems. She could use praise. She could give him some jobs that he could do, and then thank him for doing them, and praise him for doing them well. I pointed out that adults respond to this kind of treatment and that perhaps the reason she saw life in such a negative fashion was because she had experienced marital troubles and actually did not have anyone to praise her, be affectionate to her, just as I was suggesting that she be to Bobby. These ideas seemed to get through to her. No doubt this is a great need in her life and perhaps she began to recognize this a little bit.

Mrs. Schmidt then defended herself by saying that she could not change the way things were. I interrupted to suggest that she should not change things, that she should not quit her schooling and stay home with Bobby as she had suggested, and that she had to develop a different attitude. She should be more appreciative of her son and of herself and see herself in a more worthy light,—in other words, develop a better self-concept, although I did not use this term with her. The thought still persists that unless this parent changes not much hope can be held for the child.

Keeping Parents Informed

In any kind of community, the objective, realistic methods that the school uses in handling problems that arise with children and their families involve keeping parents informed. At all times the school should keep everyone who is concerned about a problem—children and parents alike—informed about what has happened and how the happenings are viewed. When the school explains to parents its ways of working with children, it is helping parents learn how to guide their children in solving their problems. This way of working is illustrated by the following incident reported by a principal in a school located in a socioeconomically disadvantaged community.

The incident is typical of the many name-calling incidents that occur with upper-grade children in any kind of community. If a child lives in a middle-class community, he is apt to have his less desirable characteristics used in the selection of his nickname: "Fatso," "Skinny," "Red." His resentment of the apt description gets him into verbal interchange and, but only occasionally, into a fist fight or a hair-pulling match. But if he lives in a deprived community he is more apt to have a nickname that tries to put him into some social category that he thinks undesirable: "Dirty Mexican," "White trash," "Nigger." The verbal interchange quickly deteriorates into physical combat.

> Jerry and Richard, two sixth-grade boys, were sent into the office for fighting on the playground. The two boys were fighting so fiercely that the other boys could not pull them apart and a teacher had to do it. Even after about five minutes of waiting in the outer office, they were still exchanging strong words. Walking into the principal's office, Jerry was saying, "You are a coward and you know it." Richard was replying that he did not want to get into trouble fighting on the playground. Then he mentioned that he would get Jerry after school.
>
> When the principal sat down, both boys started talking at once. Finally it was decided that Jerry was to talk first. He said that Richard thought himself a big shot; that he went around calling everybody "Punk" and was always picking on the little kids; that he was always saying that he was going to get them after school, but that on the way home he would run fast ahead of them and, when they followed, he would run into his house.
>
> When given his turn to talk, Richard said that Jerry was little. "Why shouldn't I call him little?"
>
> When the principal asked Richard what "Punk" meant, Richard said, "Aw, it means 'no good'."
>
> "Do you know any other meaning for it?" the principal asked, to bring out desirable as well as undesirable meanings of the word.
>
> Next the principal and the boys discussed name calling and how people felt when they were called names that they did not like. Those who call names are often those who have been called names by other people.
>
> Richard said, "Yeah, I know. All the Hawaiians called me names when I lived in the Islands." Previously he had told the principal about hating Hawaii and the Hawaiians because "they are mean and pick on Mainlanders."
>
> While the principal was answering a phone for a few minutes, Richard said to Jerry, "I'll get you after school."
>
> The principal said then, "Well, since you seem to think that a fight is the only way to settle this, perhaps we should have it and get it over with. We can have a refereed fight right here and see that it is fair and safe."
>
> Richard immediately said that he did not want to fight in the office and get into trouble.
>
> The principal reassured him that he would not be in trouble

for fighting in the office but that he would be if he were to have a fight on the playground or on the way home.

When the principal asked Jerry if he would be willing to fight in the office, he said, "Richard is a lot bigger, but I think I can take him. Anyway, I'll try."

The principal said that she would need to get consent of both parents but that she was sure that this consent would be no problem. She proceeded to call Jerry's home and was given full consent.

Richard was sure that his mother was not home.

The principal said, "Well, maybe she's back now." She called and found that the telephone was temporarily disconnected.

Richard was visibly relieved. But then the principal remembered a sixth-grade parent meeting scheduled for that evening and told Richard that she would ask his mother for her consent that evening.

The principal asked both boys if they could control their feelings until the next day when a fight could be arranged.

Richard said, "I don't want to fight and get into trouble. Let's forget about it."

The principal said, "I doubt that people forget being made fun of, but sometimes when people stop doing or saying things which hurt other people's feelings, then the hurt people know that they are trying to change and perhaps then are able to forgive."

When Jerry was asked what he thought, he said, "Well, I used to call names, but none of the kids liked me, so I quit. But I'm tired of being made fun of, especially when Richard says it and then runs. If Richard will stop, I won't fight him. But if he keeps it up, I'll get him whether we get into trouble or not."

Richard said again that he thought we should forget it.

The principal said, "Well, we can see what happens. But in the meantime I will get your parents' consent for the fight. If you need to, you can fight in the office where the fight will be refereed and there will be no spectators."

The boys agreed and left for their rooms.

The principal was glad that the boys' parents as well as the boys were seeing that problems are worked out by talking, and that boys can fight with a referee and without an audience rather than on impulse and with shouts from the crowd.

Furthering Communication

Good communication is an essential element in parent-school cooperation. In communities in which families are of different ethnic backgrounds and not proficient in speaking English, the school must minimize any difficulty in communicating with parents as well as their children, and see to it that an interpreter is readily available. Perhaps a bilingual office worker or teacher's aide can double as an interpreter. A bilingual mother can be employed to smooth out playground situations at the noon recess. A bilingual teacher or supervisor can help the school faculty understand the kinds of problems that arise in a bilingual home and in the classroom.

In the following account, a school principal reports an incident in which an interpreter was indispensable.

Clarence and Pablo, two sixth-grade boys were scuffling in the boys' lavatory. Clarence said that he was in the lavatory when Pablo came up and hit him, and that he got Pablo down on the floor and that Pablo then said, "No, no. I don't want to fight. Me no fight. Me no fight you."

Then Clarence said he let Pablo up and started out the door when Pablo booted him again, so he socked him in return.

At that point the teacher who had found the boys in the lavatory brought them to the office, and I sought ways of helping the boys learn to handle their problems in a socially acceptable manner.

I asked Pablo who hit first and he said, "I did."

When I asked how he hit, he said he played.

Recognizing the language difficulty, I sent for the interpreter to speak Spanish to Pablo and to interpret for him.

With the help of the interpreter, Pablo said that he ran into the lavatory, found Clarence, ran up to him and hit him. Then Clarence became angry and got him down on the floor and hit him several times.

Clarence intervened to say that Pablo called him "Chicken," and that was why he hit him.

I questioned this and asked Clarence to think again. I said I did not really believe that Pablo knew the word "chicken" or its connotation in our language of a person lacking in courage. I asked Clarence to see if he remembered now exactly what had happened.

Clarence then said, "Well, I guess Pablo didn't call me chicken, but it sounded like it, and he hit me first."

Pablo understood this and said, "I play. I play." Through the interpreter I talked to Pablo about how he might ask boys to play instead of coming up and hitting hard. Maybe he could ask them or wait until they were outside and play with them in a game.

We talked about how sometimes little children and puppy

dogs will jump on us or hit us to get us to play. They are not angry but just want to play.

Then I spoke to Clarence about how hard it must be for Pablo to be in school where everyone speaks a language that he does not yet understand.

When I asked Clarence why he had misrepresented the facts and had not told what actually happened, he said that he was afraid that he was going to be in trouble. He knew Pablo did not speak English and he thought that he could put the blame on Pablo and get by with it.

Clarence has just begun to assert himself and to be a lone operator. Formerly he bore the brunt of his older brother's jibes, and was encouraged to pick on little children with the older brother coming to his assistance if he were needed. Clarence's mother has called several times this year to say that she is having trouble with both the boys at home. She has asked the school to help out in any way that we can.

Pablo came to the United States from Mexico and enrolled in our school last spring. He is living with his mother in the back of the house where his mother is the housekeeper and babysitter. With a family available to help him learn English, he still understands very little and we are wondering if perhaps he may be a slow learner. However, he has been in several playground problem situations and often we think that he understands more than he lets on, although we never can be really sure. When the interpreter calls his mother to tell her about incidents like the one today, she reports that the mother appreciated the call.

The socioeconomically disadvantaged families are often those which are fatherless or motherless, immigrant or transient. They are poor and without wage-earning skills. Their descendants frequently remain within the poverty category generation after generation.

But schools can provide a way out for those who will take advantage of them. The elementary schools teach basic skills and can show children and parents that further schooling enables people of any race, creed, or background to compete with others for jobs. Schools cannot function as welfare or police agencies, but they can cooperate with such agencies.

To be effective, the schools must understand that their middle-class ways and expectations are not necessarily those of the socioeconomically disadvantaged or advantaged. Realizing the desirability of working with parents for the good of the children, they should enlist the cooperation of every parent, even those at odds with the school. To work together realistically and objectively, school and parents should keep in communication at all times.

Knowing that his responsibility is to help each child in his class to master what is to be learned, the classroom teacher must leave to other parts of the school organization much of the school interaction with less advantaged families. He depends on the counselor and principal, for instance, to work with those children who express their fears and frustrations in such extreme ways as withdrawal or persistent fighting.

Meanwhile, the classroom teacher is careful to see that less advantaged children have a secure place in the classroom group and that they have every opportunity for successful experiences in learning. He makes assignments that include what a child can do if he has no supplies, equipment, or a place for quiet study. He encourages, but does not reward, participation in family trips. He does not penalize children unable to have them. He uses class time for first-hand and simulated experiences and for learning activities in which perfect practice will make for efficient mastery.

The teacher also sees that the children from less advantaged families have definite and simple responsibilities that both help the class and have visibly satisfying results. For instance, by taking a child step by step into daily responsibility for a classroom pet, the teacher helps him feel the satisfaction of keeping the pet alive and of belonging to the class by taking part in its activities. At the same time the teacher is helping the child experience the daily responsibility that is a *sine qua non* for holding a job, and the zest of having a special identity as the Keeper of the Classroom Pet.

The teacher of a child from a less advantaged family may never meet the child's parent or guardian if he or she works through the school day and has clothing suitable for work but not for coming to school. But, nevertheless, the teacher is working with that parent or guardian in helping his child develop into a confident, capable, and realistic person able to solve the basic problems of living in the United States today.

_____ *Chapter Six* _____

WORKING
INDIVIDUALLY
WITH PARENTS_____

The schools belong to the people. The quality of education which schools provide is decided to a great extent by what school patrons and other citizens in the community desire. School people everywhere are coming to realize that the purposes of education can be realized only as parents, teachers and other members of the community enter into a close, harmonious and goal-directed relationship. If such relationships are to be effective they must be based on face-to-face contact. The teacher's assignment must be such that she has time to work as a professionally qualified person with parents concerning the developmental needs of each child.

When asked: "What is the greatest problem with which you have to cope as an elementary teacher?" teachers almost invariably say that *meeting the individual needs of children* constitutes their most challenging responsibility. The differences in children in any classroom present teachers with the necessity of making adaptations in curriculum content, instructional method, and modes of guidance to meet unbelievably wide and varied physical, intellectual, social and emotional needs.

The Relation of Home Conditions to Children's Problems

Certain home conditions contribute seriously to the problems of children. The whole child comes to school and brings the influence of his home with him. The teacher knows that the behavior of a child emerges from specific causes and that these causes are multiple, complex and interrelated. The teacher knows that every behavior of the child is a manifestation of his effort to meet a need or satisfy a basic desire.

Experienced teachers know that certain conditions interfere with the child's making a good adjustment in school and frequently prevent him from deriving the greatest benefit from the experiences the school provides. A group of well trained, experienced and deeply concerned teachers listed some of the home conditions they believed to be inimical to school progress and personality development as follows:

1. Poverty resulting in poor conditions of nutrition, housing and medical care.
2. Neglect resulting in impairment of health and moral standards.
3. Excessive authoritarianism and repression resulting in fearful and submissive behavior.
4. Favoritism resulting in jealousy among the children of a family.
5. Overindulgence leading to selfishness and other inconsiderate behavior.
6. Overly ambitious parents with unrealistic aspirations and expectancies for a child with different ideas.
7. Socially ambitious parents with major interest in their own status.
8. Overly protective parents who prevent children acquiring independence and a sense of personal responsibility.
9. Excessive stimulation due, for instance, to unsupervised use of radio and television and lack of adequate rest and exercise.
10. Transiency with consequent feeling of insecurity.
11. Employed parents with little time to maintain satisfactory parent-child relations.
12. Broken homes, which often results in outsiders being resident in the home whose influence on children may be detrimental.
13. Anxieties such as those induced by world tension and war conditions, or by uncertain parent employment or income.

14. Alcoholism and narcotic addiction of parents; poor moral conditions in the home.
15. Maintenance of mores and language of a minority culture in the home; fear of and antagonism toward the majority culture; factors which complicate the child's adjustment to basic cultural differences in the school.
16. Low level of scholastic attainment of parents; indifference regarding school attendance and achievement of children.
17. Materialistic and utilitarian life values; inconsistency in life values.

All of these unhappy conditions are reflected in the child's behavior at school and are the cause of many problems. The intensity of the resultant problem varies in degree, but all these conditions tend to frustrate the child, disturb him emotionally and render him less capable of a normal adjustment to the opportunities the school provides than his more fortunate classmates.

The importance of the teacher knowing the child's home and understanding the circumstances to which he must adjust out of school cannot be over-emphasized. Frequently, the teacher can help to compensate for some lack in the child's life. Frequently, too, the teacher can help the child to make a better adjustment to an environment he cannot change. As the child grows older, the teacher can help him to reevaluate his past experiences and work to modify the effect which previous unfortunate events may have had on his personality. Genuine understanding of a child's out-of-school life will inevitably lead to adjustments in the educational program.

A well prepared teacher should gain sufficient insight into family life in the community to be able to make suggestions as to ways in which the family life may implement the school program. The teacher will need information about the following questions:

1. What is the socioeconomic status of the community?
2. What are the occupations of the parents?
3. What are the health and welfare facilities of the community?
4. What are the recreational facilities of the community?
5. What is the political and economic outlook of the community?

6. What are the individual problems that parents are apt to have?
7. What are the attitudes of the parents toward education?
8. What are the resources of the community and of families which might implement the school program?

As teachers become increasingly sensitive to the impact of home and community conditions on the development of children, they can add their influence more effectively to the efforts of socially-minded citizens and thus improve conditions so each child will have equality of opportunity to grow up in a wholesome environment. Education must be a part of the community, not apart from the community.

Teachers are challenged to deeper personal concern and participation in social legislation involving minimum wages, decent housing, protection of children from the ill treatment which has aroused nationwide indignation and has won for itself the disgraceful appellation: "the battered child syndrome." Teachers are challenged to be vigilant concerning all legislation that directly or indirectly affects the welfare of children.

Teachers are challenged to support educational innovation contributing positively to human welfare, such as the extension of educational opportunity into the most formative period of life—the nursery school and kindergarten years. As professional people, teachers should demand a realistic family life education program, with access by students to a child development laboratory, in every junior and senior high school. Since nearly all these students will marry, establish a family, rear and educate children, experiences in a family life education program should be required in any curriculum oriented to the social needs of our times.

As professional people, teachers should voice their demands that conditions of teaching, particularly a teachable-size class, provide the time to work constructively with parents in creating the most favorable conditions in home and school for rearing and educating children. As a professional responsibility, teachers must seek to sharpen their knowledge and social skills in working effectively with mothers and fathers as well as with children.

Because negative conditions are painful to consider, human beings tend to avoid thinking about them. But as a doctor must consider conditions inimical to his patient's health, so must the teacher bring clear understanding not only to the characteristics of a home that is *good for children* but to the characteristics of a home that is *not good for children.* Teachers must have the courage to accentuate the negative as well as the positive in their own thinking and decision making.

In their face-to-face contact with parents they will be invariably honest but at the same time courteous, understanding and empathetic.

Parallel lists of characteristics are frequently helpful in contrasting positive and negative characteristics. This method of presentation follows with regard to a home that is good for a child and a home that is not good for a child:

Good for a Child	*Not Good for a Child*
1. Provides love and understanding, respect and acceptance among the members of the family	1. Exhibits rejection, repression, neglect, indifference, lack of respect, lack of affection, or hostility among family members
2. Maintains consistent standards of acceptable behavior, democratically arrived at by parents and children	2. Shows lack of respect for individual personality; discipline is erratic, authoritarian and inconsistent; unquestioning obedience is enforced by punishment
3. Provides the basic needs of food, clothing and shelter	3. Is unable to provide basic human needs to preserve life and health
4. Helps its members to live realistically in an anxious age and to grow in the capacity to accept and cope with some of the insecurities of life	4. Evades facts
5. Provides basic medical and dental care	5. Is unaware of, indifferent to, or unable to provide basic medical and dental care
6. Provides consistent and kindly adult supervision and guidance	6. Fails to provide adequate supervision and guidance
7. Stimulates the development of hobbies, provides for wise use of leisure, plans and enjoys family recreation	7. Establishes few, if any, constructive individual and family interests

Good for a Child	*Not Good for a Child*
8. Believes every child is an important member of the family group; one child is not compared unfavorably with another	8. Compares one child unfavorably with another, shows preference for favorites
9. Has realistic ambitions and aspirations for the child	9. Parents project their unfulfilled desires on their children; hold unrealistic or negative expectancies for child's achievement
10. Has reasonable certainty and permanence in place of residence	10. Is continually moving from place to place; has an uncertain future
11. Accepts and lives in accordance with the worthy ideals of the surrounding community	11. Rejects the community ideals and establishes a cultural island of its own
12. Supports each child in his quest for individuality	12. Resents behavior which makes a child an individual who is different from his parents

Fortunately, most parents and most teachers are eager to work together to help each child achieve his potential and make his best adjustment to the society in which he lives. Home visits by his teachers are essential to any genuine understanding for a child. Individual parent-teacher conferences are indispensable in bringing about the necessary mutual understanding of what both parents and teacher can do in facilitating the child's optimum development. A formal, official document may suffice to report the meter readings on gas, electricity or water consumption, or in submitting a bill for property taxes. But a formal report card is a poor substitute, indeed, for parents and a teacher sufficiently devoted to a young, dependent, human being who needs the benefits that will result from warm, wholehearted communication in which a tremendous investment of knowledge, affection, and responsibility is willingly made. Only through cooperative effort of a highly personal nature can the institution of group living contribute to human progress through the optimum development of every child.

The stake of parents and teacher in the individual conference about a child's adjustment and progress is high. If these adult guides can help a child to understand his problems and face them realistically, if he is assured that he has the love, support and security of his family and his friendly teacher, he will be able to meet life with courage, faith, self-confidence and determination to be a worthy and active citizen in his world. The expenditure of a few hours' time is surely a small investment for such a return.

The Teacher as Interpreter of the Educational Program

Whose responsibility is it to interpret the educational program to parents? Many school systems do not have a clearly defined policy concerning where this responsibility rests. As a result, many parents are left with their questions unanswered. Parents are eager to know just what teachers are doing, what experiences their children are having, what progress they are making and how parents can help.

Many phases of the educational service can best be interpreted by the administrative authority of the school system. Teachers, however, occupy key positions between the home and school. Through planned person-to-person contacts between parents and teachers, every teacher can fill a vital role in interpreting the educational program. The teacher is the person who is in direct contact with the parent, the child, and the school. Although most parents are interested in the official interpretations made by school administrators through the mass media of newspapers, school bulletins, radio, television and occasional community meetings, they realize that these interpretations are applicable to general situations, such as pupil population, buildings, budgets, special services, curriculum, guidance and the like.

Parents are concerned with individual children. They tend to interpret the educational program in terms of their child's reaction to it. They maintain faith or lose faith in the school to the degree that the teacher can give them a broad understanding of the total educational program and their child's adjustment to it. The teacher in whom parents have confidence understands the educational program, knows the characteristics of the children with whom he works, knows the kinds of curricular experiences likely to be developmental for these children and is able to present this knowledge in nontechnical terms understandable to the wide range of parents encountered in most communities. Wise administrators recognize the key role played by teachers in interpreting the educational program and keep them informed about pending educational innovations so they will not be taken unaware. In the in-service education program, the administrator provides experiences so teachers can grow in competence as key public relations persons in the school system.

The responsibility of the teacher as interpreter to parents seems to fall into four areas: (1) to help parents understand the role of the school in our democratic society; (2) to help parents understand the growth characteristics and behaviors associated with the age group with which the teacher is working; (3) to help parents understand that the educational program is based upon these characteristics and the needs of this particular group and the individual children who constitute the group; and (4) to help parents develop ways by which they can assure school success and desirable personality development for their child.

Teachers know that parents want frequent reassurance about their child. An opportunity to meet with a teacher who is thoroughly competent in the task of interpretation is a good way to establish a parent's confidence in the school.

State and national parent-teacher associations have long had as their major objective bringing home and school into close relation so that together parents and teachers may cooperate in the education of the child. Through work with the parent-teacher association in the particular school, an individual teacher can help to keep the parents' focus on the purposes of the school. If a local parent-teacher association seems unable to function effectively, the cause should be sought in the school's failure to use the association as an effective means to accomplish those beneficial results for which it was established.

The Conference with the Individual Parent

Although parents may learn much about the school through group meetings and the mass media, these alone do not satisfy parents. Mothers and fathers want to know about their individual child, his peculiarities and needs, and how he is getting along within this complex educational program. Only as parents see the development, and understand the adjustment, of their children to the educational plan do they grow in understanding of their children as individual personalities and in understanding of education as a social process. Teachers must, therefore, assume responsibility for the interpretation of each child's growth and progress to his parents. Grading and marking systems have long been recognized as ineffective means of accomplishing this purpose. They may actually obstruct the realization of the major purposes of education by emphasizing working to acquire extrinsic rewards rather than the intrinsic values of useful and meaningful learning. At best, any grading system can give only a partial evaluation of a child's progress. Too often they distort the facts because so many variables enter into a teacher's assignment of grades to the children in a class. All of the physical, intellectual, emotional and experiential differences represented in a class can never be taken into consideration in arriving at a mark or grade. A grade standard obviously cannot be applied with any degree of fairness to children who differ widely from one another in every conceivable way. Elementary school teachers must be freed from the tyranny of marks and grade standards and be given a chance to work with parents in terms of each child's individual assets, limitations, background, interests and behavior.

As has been previously emphasized, interpretation of the progress and needs of an individual child can best be made through conferences between the teacher and the parent. These contacts should not be left to chance meetings. Unless they are made a professional part of the education program, parents will not recognize their great importance. In the past, conferences with parents were casual or unplanned. Frequently they were held in a highly emotional atmosphere when a child had gotten into trouble and parents were called in as a part of the discipline procedure. Frequently, the attitudes of parents in this situation became defensive and many became permanently antagonistic because of this unfortunate experience. Instead of functioning in a supportive role to the child and his parents, this procedure distorted and disturbed the relationships of parent to child and the relationships of both to the school in ways inimical to the school's future success with the child.

A minimum of two well planned conferences with the parents of each child should be held during the school year. The first conference should be held early in the school year so that information gained can be immediately useful to the teacher in working with the child. The conference should help the teacher to become acquainted with the parents and to gain understanding of (1) the child's place in the family, his relations with his parents, his brothers and sisters, the neighbors; (2) the family's plans and aspirations for the child; (3) the child's daily routine, his interests and activities; (4) the provision the family makes for his recreation and for pursuing his interests.

For a child who has previously attended the school, the teacher may have access to some of this information in his cumulative record. But with a human being, conditions are never static and parents are the people best qualified to assess the present situation. They can provide important information on health problems, emerging interests, and changes in playmates.

Individual parent-teacher conferences consume a large amount of teacher time. To devote thirty minutes to a parent conference for each child in a class of thirty children means an expenditure of at least fifteen hours of the teacher's time. When two conferences are held during the year, thirty hours of teacher time is involved, not counting time for planning. Usually, conferences seem to take more time than the thirty minutes allocated to them.

Schools usually find that they cannot provide more than two such conference periods during the school year. In some cases, more conferences are needed concerning children who have special developmental problems so that parents and teacher may get a better understanding of the problem and work out an effective program for the child at home and at school.

The second series of parent-teacher conferences is usually held three or four months later in the school year after the teacher has had opportunity to work with the children. At the second conference the teacher can report progress and adjustment to the school and can secure the parents' reaction to any changes in the child's out-of-school behavior.

The purpose of any conference is the welfare of the child. Unless parents and teachers believe that the child's welfare can be improved by cooperative effort there would be no purpose in holding conferences.

Some school districts where parent-teacher conferences have been successfully held for many years, have had newcomers who missed the traditional report card. Although they have enjoyed the opportunity provided for the direct contact with their child's teacher, they have demanded that the school also send home periodic reports in the traditional form.

The amount of time teachers give beyond their teaching responsibilities to parent-teacher conferences probably represents the maximum amount of time which should fairly be assigned to working with parents. This fact should be made clear to parents in a group meeting in which the values to be derived from each method of reporting pupil progress are thoroughly explored and the school's position made completely clear. In planning for a parent conference, the teacher always tries

1. To keep in mind that parents are subjective and emotional about their children and that this behavior is normal and desirable. The teacher should begin the conference with a comment or an anecdote that shows that she sees the child as a person and appreciates his good qualities.

2. To help the parents see the child's emerging interests. What is new in a child's development provides clues for procedures and indicates his readiness for new activities.

3. To help the parents see growth. Parents are so close to children and are so anxious for them to progress that they sometimes fail to see their small increments of growth. If the teacher keeps anecdotal records and carefully dates each one, she can share cumulative evidence of growth gratifying to parents. Keeping a file for each child of his best spelling or arithmetic paper of the week, a series of paintings, a collection of dated compositions is most impressive. A paper saved in September provides a benchmark by which to measure a similar paper produced in February.

4. To make some causative analysis and to suggest some special procedures if a child is not adjusting to a group or making normal progress. Negative and judgmental statements about a child without analysis of the probable causes of his problem or constructive suggestions for improvement are valueless, put the parent on the defensive, and are damaging to all the human relationships involved.

A simple form that some teachers have found helpful has space for the child's name, grade, school, and district at the top with space below for four descriptions:

1. A strength, special ability, or interest.
2. Most immediate need.
3. What the teacher plans for the child.
4. What the parent plans for the child.

Such a form can be made in duplicate and signed by the teacher and by the parent. It constitutes a record in the teacher's file as she continues to work with the child, and is a commitment made by both parent and teacher to a thoughtfully considered course of action.

Chapter Seven

EVALUATING
PUPIL
PROGRESS_____

When parent and teacher sit down together to talk, they usually talk about the progress that Lucy or Tom is making, and they usually place some value on what he has been doing. In other words, they say:

> He has been doing it, or he has not been
> doing it; and this is good, or this is bad.

The discussion assumes that the teacher thinks that Lucy or Tom should be doing a particular kind of thing or should be behaving in a particular kind of way. It also assumes that the parent agrees that this objective is important.

If the parent does not agree with the importance of the teacher's objective, or does not understand what it is, he may get only one point from the conference with the teacher: The teacher does not like Lucy or Tom. In fact, the parent may go further and question whether the teacher likes any of the family. He may even decide that if the teacher does not like him, he does not like the teacher and does not like the school.

Such negative reactions are to be avoided as outcomes of attempts to evaluate pupil progress. Whatever is said or is not said, the outcome of the parent and teacher discussion, oral or written, should be a favorable feeling about the school. Support for schools by voters and legislators should not be put in jeopardy when application of mental hygiene principles in working with parents can assure favorable views about schools.

The Teacher States Objectives

Early in the fall semester, in a city school system, the Parent-Teacher Association sponsors "back to school" night for parents to meet teachers and learn the teachers' objectives and plans for the school year. The usual PTA meeting is quickly concluded with a brief orientation talk by the school principal. He welcomes the parents and introduces each member of the school staff who is available to help children and their parents in seeing that each child develops as much as possible in his studies. He invites parents to come to the regularly scheduled hour that he holds for discussing any questions that parents may have about homework and other school policies. He points out that parents need to realize that the teacher who seems most inadequate to them on first acquaintance may be exactly the kind of adult that their child needs to be with at his present stage of development. As soon as the principal concludes his remarks, the meeting is adjourned and the teachers go to their rooms to receive parents.

Each teacher has a "room mother" to welcome the other parents. She carefully pins on a name tag which serves to introduce the parent and provides him with a souvenir of the evening. Children who are at home with a sitter appreciate having the name tag as evidence of parental interest so it is usually a brightly colored fall leaf or some other attractive emblem. In fact, it often is a craft product that the children made in preparation for this welcome to their parents.

The teacher uses her room and her conversation with each parent to acquaint visitors with her objectives. "We Learn Responsibility," may be the placard above the list of "room helpers" for that week. "What We Learn," may be the title of a list that class and teacher have prepared together, stating what their objectives are. The science table, the room library of books, the evidences of planning for a class project—all attest to the fact that the class is indeed learning in keeping with its objectives.

As she talks with the parents of each child, the teacher tries to convey to them her pleasure in knowing their child and them, and her confidence in what the child will accomplish through the class work. She may know several children so well that she can emphasize an objective that is especially important for each of them. Whenever she can, she talks to parents about the few outstanding objectives for the class at its stage of development. "By the end of the year we want Jimmy to be enjoying reading. We want him to discover the fun of finding and reading books about something he is interested in," she may say. She may go on to suggest ways in which Jimmy's parents can help him. "Is there a quiet spot at home where Jimmy can read?" she may ask. Or she may suggest his staying after school sometimes to spend half an hour in the library. Or, if parent cooperation is high, she may encourage trips to the neighborhood library to use another collection of books besides the school one.

Not only at specially scheduled times, but also at other times when she meets parents, the teacher speaks of her teaching objectives. She does not take it for granted that parents will know what she is trying to accomplish with their children. Nor does she expect them simply to trust her judgment about doing what is best. She thinks of the changes that she expects to take place in the children during their school term with her, and she takes every opportunity to encourage the children and parents to work for the same changes.

The Parent Accepts Objectives

A parent has to know the objectives of his child's teacher before he can help in attaining them, or in appraising their degree of attainment. A teacher's statement about "what we are trying to do" can make the difference between helpful parents and those who are apathetic.

It is always appropriate for a teacher to explain what her class is to accomplish within the school term, or within any part of it. The clarity of her mental map about where the class is going is essential not only to her teaching but also to cooperation of children and parents in the attainment of goals.

Even when a parent is told about the school goals, he may not be sufficiently in tune with them to hear them accurately. If he is concerned about where the child's next meal is coming from, and his own as well, he is not highly receptive to information about goals that are of less immediate concern. If he is wondering about what people are thinking of him—of his shabby clothing, of his use of English, of his being different from the other parents—he may give little real attention to what the teacher is saying about her teaching objectives. It may be more important for the teacher to welcome a parent and help him feel comfortable than to immediately attempt to discuss the primary objective of school—helping a child learn.

One of the reasons that teaching in the usual middle-class community is easier than teaching in disadvantaged communities is that parents are more apt to understand teaching objectives and to share in their attainment. The teacher who can communicate with the parents of the children can explain teaching objectives for each subject area as well as for the grade level, and can feel that she has cooperation in working toward them.

The Child Accepts Objectives

When home and school are working for the same ends, the life of a child is smoother than if his home and school are working for different objectives. The child does well in school if his family plans to end its weekend so that Sunday evening is given to reading and study rather than television viewing. The parent who is more concerned that his child be a leader of a youth group than that he be a good student is apt to adversely affect the child's school achievement. But the child least apt to succeed in school is the child whose parents have no special concern with school, whose playmates in the neighborhood care less about school than other activities, and whose individual interest in school results only in poor grades and other evidence of lack of success there.

The ideal of having child, parents, and teacher all working for the success of the child in his school tasks is attained when they all gain satisfaction out of what the child accomplishes at school. Emphasizing the attainment of grade level goals and of individual goals within the reach of a child makes for his progress.

"Hate it! Hate it! Hate it!" says Susan at home after school. She opens her book, and gets her paper and pencil out on the table. "You're a lucky puppy," she says to her dog. "You don't have to do homework."

Her mother has read books on child and adolescent development. She considers Susan's behavior, rather than her words, and is not disturbed. But a mother with a different background might develop Susan's verbalism into an argument, into physical aggression, or into some other diversion from homework. Parents can reinforce, or interfere with, a child's acceptance of school objectives.

Importance of Communication

Many activities now going on in schools give evidence of the school's desire to provide better individual guidance and to improve communication with the homes they serve. In addition to the nationwide trend to provide opportunity for parent-teacher conferences, schools are attempting such additional ways of maintaining avenues of communication as these:

1. Pupils in third grade and above prepare a brief written account each Friday afternoon in which they evaluate their work and achievement for the week. These are taken home to the parents.
2. Meetings of parents are held to provide greater explanation of the meaning of marks on a written report.
3. Written reports are showing increased use of descriptive terms in evaluations.
4. Written reports are showing increased use of individual progress comments and, in the upper grades, of comparative comments.
5. Written reports are including items on personality, work habits, and social traits in reporting.
6. The combination of reporting by both parent-teacher conferences and written reports is widespread. Often the methods are alternated at six-week intervals.

Describing Pupil Progress

When school and teacher objectives are clear in the minds of child and parents as well as school personnel, the foundation is laid for describing pupil progress. At intervals throughout the school year, the teacher has responsibility for communicating to parents the nature of the progress of their child. What should be communicated and what should be the nature of the communication process? More specifically, should the teacher discuss many specific goals, or a few more general ones? Should reports be oral or written? Should attainment of goals, or progress toward them, be discussed? With what quantitative precision should pupil progress be reported? Such questions need to be considered in the light of what is known about effective communication, the roles of parents, and the role of a teacher.

A few or many goals?   The classic story is told about the small boy who wanted to know more about the stars.

"Mother," he said, "tell me about the stars."

"You ask your father about that, dear," his mother replied. "He is the one who knows about the stars."

The little boy looked disappointed and then said, "But I don't want to know that much!"

How much parents want to know about the goals of their child's teacher depends on their interests and intelligence. The interest of a mother in the goals of the teacher of her only child may be very high, especially if she is a former teacher. But if she has a background of schooling in a markedly different kind of school, or in practically no school, she may be concerned only that her child is in school as much as the attendance supervisor expects.

A principal in a community of lower social class reported that looking into the case of a boy performing below his ability level, he uncovered the probable cause—unrealistic parent expectations. The report says:

> In former years, Billy's teachers have invited his mother in for a conference regarding both his behavior and his lack of interest in school work. We have had him tested and find that he has better than average ability. Yet in most of his academic subjects he is working one or two grade levels below his actual grade level.
>
> His mother feels that Billy will outgrow his present level of achievement. She says that her brothers did not enjoy school until they got into high school. Then they became *A* students. She sees this achievement as the future for Billy too.

In conferences of parents and school personnel, the questions that a parent asks reveal his expectations, which influence the accomplishment of his child. "Is he doing all right?" may go with other comments revealing concern that the child be well thought of. "Is he doing his work?" may be the question of a conscientious work-oriented parent. "Is he going to pass?" may tie in with past experience of having a child on the lower border of the class.

The questions that a parent asks give the teacher cues as to what suggestions will extend the influence of the parent in desirable directions. A parent who asks one or two general questions can be encouraged in widening his expectations, and thinking about what his child can do further.

"You have asked about whether Jane is doing her work, and I have told you about how conscientious she is in the work she does at her seat. But I want to tell you, too, about how well she is reading. She has finished the first book that the class reads and is starting on her second book. We want her to enjoy reading and are pleased that she has a good start. Do you sometimes take her to the library?"

In most communities, responsibility for analyzing general goals to see which are of particular importance for a child rests with the teacher. A good teacher is a good diagnostician. In talking with a parent, she is able to put her finger on the goal most important for a parent to emphasize. Many a child has become a contributor to class discussion, for instance, because his teacher pointed out his need to develop in that way, and gained parent cooperation in having him report experiences he had with his family.

Occasionally a parent is also a diagnostician. When a parent asks whether the sixth-grade class has regular assignments to do at home, his question is a cue to the teacher about what parents and school can do to help sixth-grade Phillip develop better work habits.

What kinds of goals?   What kinds of goals does a teacher have, and which of these goals are important for parents to understand? The answers to these questions differ from teacher to teacher, and from community to community. A science teacher may think that pupils in the seventh grade must, above all else, develop the habit of doing what is required and handing each assignment in on time. In teaching science, therefore, he uses the written assignments as a means of developing these work habits. Since this goal is undoubtedly important in the development of children, it is important enough to be shared with the parents as well as with the children. This might be done, for instance, in a report to parents which emphasizes two goals: (1) understanding of science, and (2) handing in written assignments on time. Pupil progress then should be described and reported with regard to each of these goals separately.

A teacher needs to be aware of each major goal that he has, and to help students and parents see progress toward each of them. When goals are combined and a single report is made of them, pupils and parents are confused. For instance, when the seventh grade science teacher put together Bill's excellent understanding of the science content of the course with his failure to develop the habit of turning in written assignments as they were due, he reported a single grade of D for the course. Bill was confused by this because he had tried to understand well what was in each assignment, thinking that understanding science was the important goal. Bill's parents were confused because they had each studied science, used it in their daily work, and were accustomed to discussing at length scientific matters with Bill.

Confusion resulting from combining reports toward two or more goals may not stop with the child's family. When Bill's high scores on tests of scholastic aptitude were the basis for a scholarship to a college preparatory school, the school interpreted the D mark in science as evidence that Bill had not learned the science content of the course. The teacher who confounds goals in describing pupil progress confuses others who work with the pupil.

Actually a teacher usually has three different kinds of goals for his pupils. Progress toward each kind of goal is appraised in a different way, and should be reported separately. The three kinds of goals, and the concern of parents with each of them is as follows:

Change expected in pupils	*Parent concern with the goal*
Understands important concepts in each subject field	Can help child see how a concept is applied
Develops skills in thinking and in doing	Encourages child to use each skill
Develops attitudes and interests favorable to continued self-development	Reinforces the development of favorable attitudes and interests

What goals a teacher reports on for school records may be different from the goals that he reports on for transmittal to parents. The school records should show as accurately as possible how each child is developing in each field of study. Future teachers should not have to rediscover the nature of a child when it has been revealed by a set of scores on a series of published tests. Time is saved for teaching through the transmittal of records of progress toward school goals.

But how much of a pupil's progress should be communicated to his parents depends upon the parents' readiness to receive this communication. A policy of full disclosure of pupil progress to parents at any time should be coupled with realism about what can be communicated effectively at any one time. One school modified its reports to parents when it discovered that the parents wanted their children "to be happy," and were interpreting report cards on the basis of having their children happy on a day-to-day basis rather than on the basis of preparation for responsible adulthood.

Oral or written reports?   Extending parental goals is a likely outcome of a conference with parents; it is a less likely outcome of a written report. "Tom needs to improve his handwriting," as a statement on a report to parents may lead to the unwritten reply, "well, why don't you teach him how to do it better?" but is most apt to elicit no parent response. However, as a comment within the setting of a parent conference, the statement might easily lead to plans for a pen pal, and for frequent attention to the quality of handwriting both at school and at home.

A conference of parent and teacher adds an emotional dimension to the reporting procedure. The smile, the understanding gesture, the genuine listening in the discussion of a problem make for mutual confidence. Suggestions set within this matrix of good rapport are readily accepted. Parent action to solve a problem of a child and to further the good influence of the school is a more likely outcome of a conference than of a report card.

The conference enables parent and teacher to identify and discuss a problem to the point of planning action to remedy it. A written report is a means for teacher, or parent, or both to ignore, or put on the shelf, a matter of importance to the child. For instance, when a child is not doing as well as he has done in school, a teacher can assign low grades and think, "he has gotten lazy." The parent, receiving the written report, can say, "he got low grades this time," and can think, "I wish the teacher would give him more help. However, I know that is hard to do with the classes so large." But when parent and teacher sit down to discuss how David is doing, they are apt to discover David's basic problem. They find out that David is listless both at home and at school, and they probably will plan to have a physician examine him. With his anemia identified and remedied, David then is able to resume his good performance at school.

Frequency of reporting.   Communication between school and parents regarding pupil progress depends on the age of the children. In preschool groups, parents and teachers may have a few minutes together when the parent brings, and comes for, his child. At the conclusion of the school year, the preschool teacher and the parent take a look back over the year to see the progress that a child has made, and to plan for his future development. During the school year, the parent and teacher feel free to talk over any phase of the child's progress.

When a child enters a kindergarten or first-grade class, he often enters a large group handled by a single teacher, and his parents move into the expected role of less active participation in his school experience. The custom of reporting progress two or three times a school term is accepted as part of the tradition. It is generally understood that any unusual problem will be taken up immediately by parents and school. A teacher feels free to call a parent by telephone, and a parent feels free to get in touch with the school. But the social customs of the neighborhood will determine in some measure the frequency of communication. A mother hesitates to go to the school if her neighbors interpret her visits as "meddling" or "trouble." As she walks down the street to the school, she needs strong motivation to offset the desire to conform to what her neighbors expect.

The school that arranges for every parent to come to school to discuss the progress of his child sets up channels of communication understandable to the entire community. It is easier for a parent to come than not to come. Neighborhood expectations then reinforce communication rather than interfere with it.

Description and/or evaluation? In an effort to make a single report of pupil progress serve two purposes, schools are apt to overlook the fact that what is an effective means of internal communication within the school system may not be an effective means of communication outside the school system. What makes an effective school report may not make an effective parent report. Many middle-class communities have enough school people among them to justify using school reports as parent reports also, but this fact has too long obscured the fact that many communities need to have parent reports of a different nature.

A school person is trained to use information about where a child has ranked in his previous class in a particular study, or about how much improvement he was able to make during the term, or about how well he has mastered the work in that study. But parents, who are not so trained, are better able to use descriptions of how a person behaved in a particular situation. Any parent can understand that a child did not hand in a notebook, but not every parent can understand a teacher's evalution that his child did D work.

An article entitled "Questions Parents Ask"[1] contrasts the written

[1] Helen Heffernan, "Questions Parents Ask," *Grade Teacher*, 81:22, 105–7 (May, 1964).

evaluation on a report card with the description at a conference between parents and teachers as follows:

> Yesterday Timmy Thomas brought home his report card. . . .
> Mrs. Thomas took the card with her usual puzzled expression.
> Timmy had an S in reading and an S in oral expression but he had an I in spelling and a U in arithmetic. Mrs. Thomas knew that S meant satisfactory but she asked herself: "Satisfactory for what? Does that mean he reads as well as others in the class? Or, considering Timmy as the boisterous active little boy he is, does it mean satisfactory for him? The I means improving. Well, I should hope so. . . . That is what he is going to school for, isn't it?"

> These marks were really meaningless to Mrs. Thomas. She did not know the basis on which the teacher had arrived at these judgments. The symbols on the report card shed no light on her questions about Timmy's progress in school.

> Some schools . . . have broken with tradition entirely. In these schools, parents visit the classrooms, and teachers help them to understand the work in progress. The parents have regularly scheduled conferences with the teachers in which the progress of the child is discussed. Samples of the child's work, the results of standardized tests, and written descriptions of the child's behavior provide the scientific and objective data for these conferences.

> Timmy's parents and teacher will leave a face-to-face conference with some positive and mutually acceptable courses of action. Parents will feel "in" and not "out" of their son's education. They will recognize that education is a joint enterprise in which parents and teacher play supportive roles in the drama of Timmy's becoming the finest human being he is capable of becoming.

Pupils and parents both are better able to use description than evaluation of the progress a pupil is making. If a pupil knows that he has not been writing neatly, and that his teacher expects him to hand in each paper written neatly, he is in a position to do something about improving his work. But if the pupil knows only that he is doing C work, he can only guess about what to do. He may find it easier to guess that the teacher, rather than he, ought to do things differently, or to rationalize the C on the basis of just not being good in school work.

Parents find description more useful than evaluation of progress by use of symbols. Knowing how their child is behaving and how he is expected to behave, the parents can help their child behave more often as he is expected to. Instead of a vague evaluation such as *B,* the parents have a definite objective with which to work. Both they and their children then have a better chance for real progress toward school goals.

Labeling or lending a hand? In an effort to absolve themselves of feelings of guilt about low pupil performance, a teacher is sometimes tempted to end his responsibility for helping a pupil by putting a derogatory label on him. This temptation becomes greater as the number of pupils in the class increases. The teacher of large classes in a tax supported school which carries on the tradition of a five-point grading scale, finds it easy to sort pupils into five different categories and to work effectively with one or two of the categories while the other categories remain as labeled.

But the teacher who knows the behavior to be developed in his pupils and knows how to observe pupil behavior can describe how a pupil is doing. His descriptions are valuable as a basis for effective teaching of the pupil not only at school but also at home. The descriptions of the teacher combine readily with descriptions of parents, and form an objective background for diagnosing what a pupil needs to help his progress in school work.

Remarks of teachers and parents reveal their beliefs about children and their ability to help them. In the following lists are remarks often found associated with "labeling," and other remarks with "lending a hand."

Labeling	*Lending a Hand*
If a boy is a nuisance in class, I grade him down.	He needs to learn how to help others instead of bothering them.
He scores high on intelligence tests but low in class work. Let's put the heat on and see if he brings his grades up.	I wonder what factors go with his low grades in class work; his intelligence test scores indicate ability, so some other factor must make for low performance.
He is new in the school, so he has a lot to learn before he gets good grades.	As the class is reviewing its last work, he makes a list of what he does not know and gets my help with each item.

Some Questions About Appraisal

From time to time parents as well as professional educators raise questions about each part of the educational process. The appraisal of pupil progress comes in for its share of their attention. Basic concepts about appraisal should be so well understood by everyone working with children and their parents that simple explantions can be given at any time. Here are some common questions together with some simple answers:

> *Question:* Should schools report to parents about pupil progress?
>
> *Answer:* Yes.
>
> *Discussion:* The entire teaching process depends on knowing changes to be expected in pupils as a result of the classroom experiences. To be able to help the class as a whole and to help the individuals within the class group, a teacher has to know how far each pupil has progressed. In fact, to know how effective teaching is and how to improve teaching, a teacher has to know how pupils are progressing.

The question, then, about whether schools should report to parents about pupil progress is really the question of whether teachers should report to parents what they know about the progress their children are making toward the goals the teacher has for them.

The answer to that question is "yes," because parents and teachers help children more when they reinforce each other. If Miss Smith at school is showing Jerry Johnson the fun of reading, and Mrs. Johnson at home is encouraging Jerry to enjoy reading, Jerry is going to learn the pleasures of reading more quickly than he would if only Miss Smith, or only his mother, is helping him. Even if Mrs. Johnson does not enjoy reading, she can encourage Jerry to learn it if Miss Smith shows her how fortunate Jerry is in making use of advantages that were not available to everyone twenty or more years ago.

The answer to the question about whether schools should report to parents about the progress of their children is "yes," too, becasue parents pay for the education of their children, directly in private schools, and indirectly in public schools supported by tax money. The continued existence of schools depends on the confidence of parents and other supporters of schools, and their confidence depends in turn on evidence that schools are doing what they purport to do. Reports to parents about pupil progress build and maintain confidence.

Question: What should schools report to parents about their pupils?

Answer: The schools should report to parents what they want to know, and what they should know.

Discussion: What parents want to know is that their child is making progress toward becoming the adult they want him to be. Recognition of the development of their child is evidence that they are successful parents.

A feeling of success as a parent contributes to his success as a parent. His confidence in himself and in his child in their relation to the school is apt to influence the relationship itself. From this fact it follows that a school should report to a parent some real progress that a child is making. If a teacher cannot report progress for a particular child, that child should have another teacher. A child who is physically well should be developing noticeably in at least one area of his life. It is the responsibility of the teacher to show that development to the child's parents.

Sometimes a child's progress is so much less than the progress made by most of the children in his school group that his teacher suggests his transfer to another group. In working with the parents in making such arrangements, the school is careful to emphasize that the child is progressing and that the transfer is being made only to facilitate his further progress.

In addition to reassurance about the progress of their child, parents need to know some one area in which they can work with the school in helping their child. At the least, parents can help their child appreciate the opportunity of going to school. At the most, they can give specific assistance in some curricular subject—perhaps giving their child practice with arithmetic combinations through the use of flash cards. The kind and amount of help to be expected differs from social class to social class. In a fragmented family, for instance, parental resources may be greatly extended in providing minimal food, clothing, and shelter. Or in a family whose head is the manager of the principal industry of the community, parental attention may be almost wholly diverted from the children. In a family having someone who has studied the learning process, that adult can effectively supplement the child's teacher. Furthermore, the school-oriented middle-class family provides its children with a climate favorable to achieving school objectives.

Question: Should the school report to parents orally or in writing?

Answer: Reporting both orally and in writing is preferable to reporting by either method alone.

Discussion: Communication between school and parents is so important that the use of two channels of communication is desirable. If communication has to be limited to one means, in most instances verbal communication is desirable since it offers opportunity for school and parents to talk together about problems concerning the child. However, a private school serving families of busy professional and executive people will probably find written communication especially suitable.

Oral communication is essential with families that make limited use of materials printed in English. In communities in which most parents work, the school may wish to set up parent conference times available for those who work night shift, as well as conference times for those whose working hours are similar to the hours usually kept by school people.

Other parts of this book, especially Chapter Two, deal with parent conferences in detail.

Question: In reporting pupil progress, is it preferable to use descriptive statements, or marks?

Answer: In the elementary school, it is preferable to report pupil progress to parents with statements that describe pupil behavior.

Discussion: In the elementary school, emphasis is on pupil improvement, and descriptions of behavior easily communicate what parents need to know. In secondary schools, a second emphasis becomes important as prospective employers and admission officers of higher schools need to find the young people especially fitted to their situations. At that point, descriptions of behavior can be supplemented by marks that show where a student stands in relation to others in his class group.

Question: Should schools report to parents children's scores on standardized tests as well as teacher-made tests?

Answer: The school should share with parents whatever evidence it has about the progress of each child toward the goals that school and parents have for the child.

Discussion: Standardized tests should be selected in relation to the school objectives. Both teaching and testing are in terms of changes expected in the behavior of pupils. Progress in achieving each objective is made clear to the teacher and, through her, to the parents and their children. Products of school work, adult observations of child behavior, response to oral and to written tests—all such evidence is useful in communicating to parents the progress that the teacher sees in each pupil.

It is easy to determine what standardized tests are available for helping to appraise pupil progress. *The Mental Measurement Yearbook* developed by Oscar K. Buros lists published tests, describes in detail what is to be appraised by each test, and cites evidence concerning whether the test is a valid test of what it is designed to appraise.

Data about how a child compares with other children of his age and grade level are especially useful when a child enters a school new to him. At that time his scores on standardized tests enable the school to place him in a group whose academic performance is comparable to his, or to make other arrangements to facilitate his progress.

Question: In working with parents, what use should a school make of intelligence test scores?

Answer: The school should help parents of gifted children to appreciate their potential, and should help parents who belittle their children to become more realistic about them.

Reporting that intelligence test scores are above average, average, or below average is a means of helping such parents. So is giving information about the subscores which were his high scores and may indicate talents to capitalize on.

Discussion: The use of technical information depends on the ability of people to use it. Yet fear that a particular parent may misinterpret an intelligence test score of his child should be tempered with recognition that other parents may be highly trained and experienced in the use of such data, and that parents can easily learn from counselors and administrators how to interpret a test score with due recognition of what it does, and does not, show.

When a parent comes to school to ask about the intelligence test score of his child, he usually has some underlying reason for his inquiry. The following conversation between the school counselor and Mrs. Dvorak illustrates such a situation:

Mrs. Dvorak: Good morning. I am Jean Dvorak's mother. I understand that you can give me her intelligence test score.
Counselor: Good morning, Mrs. Dvorak. Yes, we do have that kind of information about our pupils, as well as other useful data about them. Tell me what is on your mind, and let me see what information we have to help with the problem.

The counselor may find, as the conversation continues, that Mrs. Dvorak is looking only for reassurance to give her daughter who is seated back of a girl who turns around to say, "I'm smarter than you are." Or she may find that Mrs. Dvorak is personally concerned about having a daughter who goes to college, and wants to be assured that her daughter has such ability. In other words, the counselor should be alert in finding out what fears or problems, if any, are associated with the inquiry for a particular test score. Then parent and counselor can go on to constructive plans and action for the good of the child. Comparisons of test scores with those of other children would, of course, be contrary to sound school policy.

Chapter Eight

SECURING
PARENTAL
INVOLVEMENT____

For years, people have known that involvement and participation are the keys to the development of interest that results in action. It is impossible to comprehend how schools can achieve their objectives for children unless parents are so close to the school that it is a part of their daily lives.

In urban areas where schools draw great numbers of children from a large region, it calls for definite planning to secure this close relationship. The plan must provide for continuity in activities year after year and for consistent evaluation to determine its effectiveness. The plan must also take into consideration the homes, neighborhood, or community from which the children come. Inherent in any successful plan for parental involvement in the educational program must be recognition of the wide range of circumstances, relationships and values represented in nearly every individual school.

A Verbal Model of a School Child's Life

School personnel used to think of the children with whom they work as coming from a middle-class family situation. Many still conceive of an elementary school child's day as beginning with his mother cheerfully awakening him, giving him what assistance he needs in selecting and putting on clean and suitable clothing, and preparing and serving for him a breakfast that gives him one-third or more of the nutrients which he needs for his day. They may think of mother as waving good-by as the child joins other children walking to school companionably. And this model is still true of many homes.

The middle-class model of a child's life pictures the child greeted by his teacher and taking his place in a group of children large enough to afford both the stimulus of interaction with other children and opportunity for learning cooperation and democratic behavior, but also small enough to provide the attention that the child needs for optimum learning. The child's school day includes an excellent school lunch that provides an additional third of a day's food properly in balance. At the end of the school day, the child returns home leisurely and safely, or is picked up by his mother to go to a special group or individual lesson of a religious, aesthetic, or recreational nature. Depending upon the weather and the length of the daylight, the child will play out of doors either by himself or with congenial companions. When his father comes home, the child enjoys being with him, while mother prepares dinner for the family.

The afternoon and evening for the family with a middle-class style of life is long enough to include guidance of the child in homework, in practice of a musical instrument, or in activities related to a current hobby. Going to bed at an hour suitable for obtaining the sleep needed at his age concludes the child's day.

The program in many schools is predicated upon such a day. The teacher is expected to provide for each pupil the help that he needs in his studies as he needs it. This assumption has continued to be made at the same time that school districts have increased the number of pupils in a classroom as a means of minimizing costs. Many schools throughout the country are now having to consider if there are more effective ways to expand and to utilize their professional staff.

Any child who needs more teacher attention than is available in the large group situation is referred to a counselor or, in a smaller school system, directly to an administrator. Conferences are arranged with the parents of the child, and the school and the parents work together until the child is again functioning adequately within a class.

As long as the basic assumptions underlying this verbal model of a child's life are not markedly different from the actuality of his life, the school program runs smoothly and the children progress regularly through it. When the individual pattern of a child's development deviates from the usual pattern, his behavior catches the attention of his teacher, and plans for helping him are worked out with parents. But in the urban setting of today, the assumptions about the life of a child may be so different from the facts that the schools must give serious consideration to setting up not one, but a series of models of the lives of children and devising school adaptations appropriate for helping all children grow up to be effective citizens. Many program variations are being tried out.[1] Each program involving parents needs to be evaluated in terms of models of the actual lives of children.

One of the models of the life of a school child today is that of the child whose mother works. The married woman is well established in the working force and is a major component of the one-third that is female. She may step out of the labor force while she is getting the family established, but she is present again in large numbers between the ages of 35 and 54. In some elementary school districts the number of mothers who work full time may be sufficiently large to have the school plan its program in terms of them. In other districts, the working mother may have part-time work which enables her to be at home with her child, or children, much of their out-of-school hours. In certain urban school districts, the number of mothers who are also heads of families may be large enough to necessitate programs of after-school care, recreation, and study for the children. In contrast to the economically advantaged two-income families, the families headed by a mother are apt to be below the poverty level, and without funds to devote to child care.[2]

In building a model of the lives of the children whose mothers work, the school needs to consider many factors. If the mother leaves for work before the children leave for school, who takes responsibility for seeing that they have breakfast each school morning, and that they are neatly dressed in keeping with the clothing of the other children in school? Who sees that they have a lunch to eat or money to buy a school lunch, and that they are in good health and are not endangering the health of others?

If the mother is employed after the time that school is dismissed in the afternoon, what arrangements are there for the children to play, work,

1 *Programs for the Educationally Disadvantaged,* Washington, D.C.: Office of Education, U.S. Department of Health, Education and Welfare, 1963.
2 Catherine Chilman and Marvin B. Sussman, "Poverty in the United States in the Mid-Sixties," *Journal of Marriage and the Family,* 26:399–405 (November, 1964).

or study under supervision until she returns from work? Does the mother have time and energy for supervising homework, and is she able to provide each child with a place to study?

The school program and the out-of-school daily routine of a child must dovetail if the child is to progress well in school. For the good of the children, the school may need to make innovations in its program, and may take a leadership role in encouraging community responsibility for meeting the needs of children whose lives deviate widely from the middle-class model.

Family Life Models for Parent Programs

In working with parents, the school needs to keep in mind the family patterns of living which predominate among the families which it serves. Many school programs involving the cooperation of parents have failed because they were based on assumptions about family life rather than actual models. Meetings should be scheduled and plans for parent participation in school events should be arranged not only in terms of the school day of the teacher but also in terms of the timing of parental responsibilities.

An elementary school should plan parent conferences with teachers, counselors or other administrators, on the basis of information about the hours that the father works, the hours that the mother works, and whether a preschool child must be taken care of during the parents' attendance at an individual conference or group meeting. Many schools have worked out satisfactory arrangements for care of young children by volunteer service of older children with adult supervision.

All kinds of arrangements are developed to meet family situations. An elementary school in a community in which many mothers have children in parent participation preschool groups makes a point of scheduling mothers' meetings or parent conferences at hours when the preschool groups are not in session. A school which has a considerable proportion of mothers who are heads of families has developed a system of evening telephone calls to mothers who work a daytime shift or whose office hours are from 8 A.M. to 5 P.M. Each school is confronted with the necessity of making arrangements for parent meetings and for individual parent conferences in terms of the availability of the parents of the children currently enrolled. Teachers who have come to value the results with the children are usually willing to make some adjustments in their own schedules to maintain close contact with parents.

Induction of Children into School

When the children enter school for the first time is the best opportunity to establish the parents' role in the educational program. For many years, school systems that provide kindergarten education have used a variety of ways to assist parents in helping their children to take successfully this first big step into school life.[3]

Schools sometimes make provision for parents with children who will be entering in the fall to attend a session of kindergarten and to bring the new kindergarten child with them. Two or three parents with their children may be asked to come on the same day. The children are invited to join in any activities of the kindergarten that appeal to them but, if they prefer to sit close to their mothers and observe what is going on, this behavior is accepted without teacher or parent urging them to participate. At the close of the session, the teacher has a few minutes with parents and children to thank them for visiting, to express her pleasure in the opportunity to become acquainted, and to tell each child that she is looking forward to his coming to kindergarten.

Teachers report that these "get acquainted" sessions are most valuable in facilitating the child's adjustment to school. He has time after the visit to think about what he has seen, to ask his parents questions, and to prepare himself psychologically for the approaching time of his own active participation as a kindergarten child.

A general meeting of parents whose children will enter school in the fall is usually held before school closes in the spring. If possible, these meetings are held in the actual kindergarten the child will attend, so parents can see the environment of the classroom and the play areas where their child will be. The kindergarten teacher, the school principal, or a consultant in early childhood education from the central office talks briefly about the characteristics of five-year-old children and about the educational program planned for the kindergarten year. Parents are encouraged to ask any questions not involving the special needs or problems of individual children. They are asked to reserve questions of this nature

[3] *The First Big Step,* "A Handbook for Parents Whose Child Will Soon Enter School," Washington, D.C. National School Public Relations Association, 1201 Sixteenth Street, N.W., 1966.

for a private conference time at the conclusion of the meeting. At no meeting is the problem of an individual child made a topic for general discussion. The personality of every child is regarded with the same dignity accorded to other human beings by courteous people.

In certain school districts, the parent-teacher association of each school cooperates with the school staff in conducting what some communities call "the summer roundup." On a schedule that is well advertised in advance, parents may bring their child entering kindergarten (or first grade child in districts that do not provide kindergarten education) to the school for medical, dental, vision, hearing or other examinations included in the local program. In certain districts, required vaccinations and immunizations may be secured at the same time.

Parents are informed about corrections which should be made during the summer so the child will start school in the best physical condition possible. Such careful checkups may also reveal conditions which help teachers to adjust the program of school activities to the individual child's needs.

Socially-minded parents from the neighborhood willingly volunteer their services to assist in scheduling appointments, in providing transportation when necessary, and in securing height and weight data for each child in order to economize on the time and energy of the doctors and nurses in attendance. Incidentally, parents who participate come to have a deeper understanding about the school's concern for the health and well-being of every child and to realize that each child receives special consideration from the teacher in terms of his individual needs.[4]

The importance of the procedure used in inducting the young child into school is so great that much of his future success can be traced to the wisdom of the adults who develop these plans. Ideally, the child should be inducted very gradually into this new experience; he should feel that he is moving for a few hours each day into a homelike place enriched by the presence of other children, friendly adults, and a creative environment which will challenge his interest. The time available, however, is unfortunately limited. Since parents can do many things in advance of the child's entrance to insure a good start, the school has a responsibility to provide them with the best possible advice based on study and experience.

Throughout the United States, schools usually prepare a printed or

[4] Helen Heffernan and Vivian Edmiston Todd, *The Kindergarten Teacher*. Boston: D. C. Heath & Company, 1959.

mimeographed bulletin of specific suggestions. One of these bulletins, prepared by a mother who was also a well trained professional consultant in the field of early childhood education, is included here as an illustration.[5] Parents who follow the wise counsel given, play a most strategic role in launching their child successfully in his new adventure.

Helping Your Children Be Ready for Kindergarten

Four and three-fourths by September first! The doors of kindergarten will open for your child.

He will be excited. So will you. And so will the twenty-some other children in his class.

He may be a little bit anxious. You may be too. And so may be the other four- and five-year-olds who are stepping out from home into the world of school.

The step from home to school should be a happy and successful step. The school people will help your child like and succeed at school.

LOVE HIM. . . .

A child is life's greatest gift. No one else has a child just like yours. He is a very special person. No other child could take his place.

Your child will grow on love and praise. He will feel secure. He will like himself. This is very important. For as he likes himself and as he feels secure, he will be able to accept and to like other people. He will be confident in reaching toward new experience.

GUIDE AND SUPPORT HIM. . . .

Your child needs the guidance of mature adults—the company of other children. He needs to be praised for his successes—supported and directed in his failures. He is nurtured by a friendly, supportive, challenging world.

PHYSICALLY. . . .

Be sure that your child is as well and as strong as possible when school begins. A physical examination during the spring or early summer will allow time to correct many health problems before school opens. Some-

---

[5] (Mrs.) Alice Krehbiel, *Helping Your Child Get Started in Kindergarten.* San Bernardino, California. Office of County School Superintendent. 1961.

times, physical examinations are offered during the school's spring "roundup."

Have a dentist inspect and clean your child's teeth and make necessary repairs.

See that your child has plenty of nourishing food, vigorous exercise out of doors, fresh air, comfortable and undisturbed sleep, and water—water to bathe in, to brush his teeth, to wash in, to drink.

Teach and encourage him to practice good habits of health and safety.

Dress him in sturdy, washable clothing, appropriate to the weather.

EMOTIONALLY. . . .

Love him.

Praise him when he succeeds; comfort and support him when he fails.

Remember that success builds confidence. A confident person seeks new experience. Through worthwhile experience comes wholesome growth.

Set limits and be consistent in helping your child to live within them.

Realize that anger and hostility are natural emotions. Give him outlets for them—clay to punch, nails to pound, room in which to run and shout.

Use "can" more than "can't;" "do" more than "don't." But do not overindulge him. He must learn that he cannot always get his own way or have everything he wants.

Make no promises which you cannot keep.

Make no threats which you should not keep.

Set aside a time each day to give him your undivided attention.

Give him time to express his thoughts; give him your attention when he talks.

Read to him—fanciful and imaginative stories, nursery rhymes—some from picture books, some from books without pictures.

Enjoy his bodily response to music and rhythm.

Sing with him; encourage him to sing.

Make listening to music a part of your family life.

Provide a variety of art materials for his use; give him freedom to create with them.

SOCIALLY. . . .

Realize that he wants to be liked, to get along well with other people. He will do his best, but he needs much help.

Be friendly. Your child will reflect your feelings and your actions toward others.

Be courteous. Your habit of using simple expressions of courtesy will rub off on him.

Remember that playmates are important—but not too many at a time nor for too long at one time. And don't be surprised if he plays *beside* rather than *with* other children of his own age part of the time, or if he seems to ignore them altogether.

Arrange for him to play at other children's homes for short periods of time without you.

Encourage "Grandmother" or "Aunt Meg" to invite him to spend the night at her house. Before he goes, help him to decide one or two things to do for his hostess.

Give him a chance to help you with some of your daily chores.

Encourage conformity to socially acceptable behavior; it facilitates cooperation.

Encourage creativity; it fosters individuality.

Remember that your youngster is not a "little gentleman" or a "little lady." He is a child. Let him live as one.

Talk with him about the help which your family receives from the milkman, the laundryman, the repairmen who come to your house.

Teach him never to accept a ride with a stranger.

INTELLECTUALLY. . . .

Remember that your child wants to learn—about people, places, events, and things. The more he learns, the more he will want to know.

Encourage him to ask questions, to experiment, to observe.

Answer his questions simply and honestly.

Take him to places where he can see things happening.

Read to him.

Censor the programs which he watches on television; limit the time he watches.

Get him a pet; be sure that he gives it proper care.

Ask him questions; really listen to his replies.

Read short and simple informative items to him.

Give him some toys and games which challenge his thinking.

Help him to become aware of texture, color, and form in natural and man-made objects.

Help him to plant flower and vegetable seeds and to care for the plants which grow from them.

Take him to the dairy to see the cows milked, the milk pasteurized and bottled; to the supermarket, the bakery, the nursery, the railroad depot. Tell him the names of the people, things, and actions which he observes.

Encourage him to retell stories which you have read or told to him.

Be sure that he can say his name and address distinctly. Many kindergarten children know their phone numbers too.

Answer his questions about measures when he helps you cook.

Answer his questions about prices when he goes shopping with you.

LET HIM GROW. . . .

It may be hard for you to let your child grow up. Yet, helping him to develop wholesome independence is your democratic responsibility.

Remember that your youngster is a unique individual. Do not try to mold him into the child you would have liked to have been. Do not try to make him be like someone you have known. He deserves the privilege of growing in his own way.

Give him a few simple jobs to do; see that he does them well.

Keep your supervision of his play and work activities as unobtrusive as possible.

Let him and his playmates resolve their own squabbles. Step in for safety's sake, if you must.

Explain the reasons behind rules; be patient with him if he breaks one.

Be sure that he has ample time during the day to use as he wishes.

Give him a small allowance to spend as he chooses.

Provide clothing which he can manage.

Expect him to dress himself—with an occasional assist from you.

Help him learn how to take care of his clothing, toys and books.

Teach him to recognize his own school clothing. Label each article.

Be sure that he knows how to use the toilet, how to wipe himself, that he routinely washes his hands after toileting.

Let him decide what he will tell you about events which happen out of your presence. Listen but don't probe.

LEARN WHAT KINDERGARTEN IS. . . .

Your child will probably get his first ideas about kindergarten from you.

How can you understand the goals and activities of the kindergarten?

Go with your child when the teacher invites all of "next year's class" to visit. Watch the children in "this year's class" at work and play. Listen to the teacher tell about the activities. Ask questions.

Read. The teacher will recommend books, pamphlets, magazine articles. She may even have some to loan to you. The librarian will help you too.

From these sources you will learn enough to assure your child that kindergarten will be a delightful place. His teacher will like him. There will be children to play with. He will make friends with many of them. Together they will work and play with the many toys and tools and with the equipment and materials in the indoor and outdoor kindergarten areas. They will grow physically, socially, emotionally and intellectually.

THAT IMPORTANT FIRST DAY. . . .

You know that kindergarten will offer your child a worthwhile experience. Your child looks forward to it. Here are some tips which should help to smooth his first day.

If he attends afternoon session, discourage his playing hard in the morning.

Have him brush his teeth.

Allow plenty of time for washing or bathing, for toileting and dressing. Tuck a cleansing tissue in his pocket.

Serve him a nourishing meal and give him time to eat it as slowly as he desires.

Take him to the bus stop or to school. If you cannot go with him, send him with a dependable older child. When he leaves you, smile, and wave good-by.

Be sure that he and his teacher know how he is to come home. A note to the teacher, pinned to your child's clothing, will help.

If your child needs money for mid-session milk or fruit juice, seal it in an envelope on which you have written the child's and the teacher's names and the amount of money enclosed. It may be wise for you to fasten the envelope to the child's clothing.

Leave your child in the teacher's care at school, unless he needs to have you stay with him a short time. His teacher will help him to find something interesting to do.

Welcome him home. If you cannot be there, make sure that someone whom he knows will be at his home when he arrives.

Listen to his remarks about school, but don't pry.

Invite him to "tell you" about the drawings, paintings, or other materials he brings home. Enjoy them with him.

Indeed, to be a four- or five-year-old in school can be a thrilling experience. So many new things to do. So many people to know. And at home—such loving, supporting, encouraging parents.

.   .   .   .   .

Such a bulletin as the foregoing can be introduced at the spring meeting to which are invited parents of children who will enter in the fall. Careful presentation of the bulletin will help parents understand that although the school's objectives and the home's objectives for the child may be expressed in different terminology, they are essentially identical. Good schools and good homes strive to increase each child's emotional security, stimulate his intellectual development, extend his social skills and relationships, and provide for his health and safety. When school, home, and community are in agreement on these basic goals, mutual understanding and cooperative endeavor directed toward their achievement are fostered.

Since it is of the utmost importance that all parents receive such a bulletin, a careful check should be kept of the parents who attend the meeting, and an effort should be made to see that other parents of new kindergarten children receive it. A copy may be mailed to parents with an appropriate letter containing a further invitation to plan a conference with the teacher before the close of the school year if this is at all possible. Unless some record is made, parents who are most in need of the guidance the bulletin strives to provide may fail to know of its availability.

Many districts set aside a week before the opening of school for the registration of entering children. During these days, parents bring their children so that both may meet the teacher together. Sufficient time is available for the teacher to get acquainted with each child, to show him the materials and equipment he will use in school, and to talk with him and his mother about the routine of the school day. This carefully planned visit lessens the apprehension nearly every young child experiences about leaving his home and entering the new world of school. Knowing the teacher informally and becoming acquainted with the school in company with their mothers help most children to feel more secure and comfortable.

While this practice is used most frequently by nursery school and kindergarten teachers, it would be equally appropriate and useful in helping older children begin the new school year with greater feelings of assurance and security. A school wishing to build close relationships with the parents could initiate such a program in the kindergarten and first grade and continue it year by year as the children move along through their school lives. This method of school registration would in five or six years become accepted procedure by children, parents, and teachers. The avenues of person-to-person communication need to be opened and kept open between teachers and parents during the entire elementary school life of the child.

What Parents Want to Know About a Child's School Progress

"How is my boy doing in school?" is the most frequent question addressed to teachers whenever they meet a parent. The question carries the parent's hope and pride and anxiety. It has no easy answer. Parents are not satisfied with "Jimmie is getting along just fine!" or "Harry is having a little trouble with mathematics."

What the parent really wants to know is how does my boy compare with other children in the class? Is he bright, average, or slow? What can we expect he will be as a man? What talents has he? What weaknesses? Is he learning as well as can be expected?

These questions seem direct, straightforward and reasonable. Surely any intelligent teacher who spends five or six hours a day with Jimmie and Harry and thirty or so other children like them should be able to give satisfactory answers. But, of course, answers to such questions are nearly impossible to give because there is so little that is absolute about a child. To say that a child is bright or dull, talented in music, or slow to read may be true one day and untrue the next. Because a baby walks two months earlier than the average baby is no guarantee that he will be a better walker at age twelve or twenty. Tests are available which reveal extreme retardation or unusual talent but in the regions between, too many variables exist for the teacher to answer the questions with any degree of reliability.

Because many parents are insistent on getting "answers" about their children's progress in school, it has been customary to send home "report cards." Because this is a required function of the teacher, she does the best she can with the bits of evidence she has at hand but no thoroughly competent teacher ever believed her evaluation to be anything more than a rough approximation of her perception of the child.

Advising About Summer and Out-of-School Activities

A positive service frequently much appreciated by parents is a book list for summer reading which appeals to children of elementary school age. With children's libraries becoming more widely available with professionally trained children's librarians on hand to help in selection, the problem of getting the right book to the right child has greatly lessened. However, in many school districts, particularly in small towns and in rural areas, the need for guidance of summer reading still affords an opportunity for parents and teachers to work effectively together in behalf of children.

A skill is perfected through practice and the skill of reading is no exception. Unless a child finds reading one of the delights of his summer holidays, he is likely to return to school in the fall with some loss in his reading ability. On the other hand, it has been found that if a child reads about twenty books at his reading level, he will actually advance his reading ability by a year. It is a truism that we learn to read by reading.

During the period when the child is free from the responsibilities of a regular school program he may extend his individual interests in science, history, travel or fiction. He can return to school in the fall reinforced with many new ideas to which he has been able to devote more time and thought than is possible in the usual crowded school schedule.

In many communities people are interested in children's literature, writers and former librarians as well as teachers. Most worthwhile parent-teacher association activities have committees that include such persons as well as children's librarians employed in the area. Such a committee might set for its goal the preparation of lists for summer reading with titles categorized by age and subject interest. Incidentally, the involvement of such a committee increases public awareness of school and local library resources and needs. Sometimes library services limp along unsupported by the public because no one has devised a way by which the public may become informed through actual involvement in meeting a real community need.

At a community meeting, the mother of five boys enrolled in the elementary school and nearby junior high school told how she and her husband had reinforced their children's learning experiences. The family income was exceedingly limited but, at least, these parents were not *poor in spirit*. They took their children on field trips to the zoo, the aquarium, the farm, the harbor, art galleries—"every place where no admission was charged," she said.

They had a copy of a list prepared by the school district on *Interesting Places to Go* and found it most useful in their early exploring. Soon they were watching the newspapers for announcements of exhibits, new buildings under construction, and festivals which were open to the public. Sometimes the family walked with the baby in a stroller; occasionally they used their car. A few excursions even involved short train trips. Making picnic lunches came to be a fine art especially when two meals were required on the trip. The excitement of living in this family was reflected as the mother told of the plans they made, what they saw, and the astonishing things they learned.

This mother explained that she was married after completing junior college and working a few years as a typist. During the years she has reared and educated her active family of boys, she has taken advantage of the opportunities the local state college afforded to complete her work for the B. A. degree and is now launched in graduate study leading to a teaching credential to qualify her as a secondary school teacher of English.

Her purpose in giving the group this information was to report how she used her college experiences to enrich the lives of the children. Her knowledge in arts and crafts was passed on to the boys who enjoyed using clay, papier-maché, finger paint, colored chalk and water colors. The home provided a supportive climate for all kinds of creative expression. The father, a skilled craftsman, helped the boys to build a tree-house, to set up gymnastic equipment, to build a basketball backboard, to construct animal cages, and eventually a boat.

Money available for presents was spent for carefully selected books, magazines, newspapers, rhythm instruments, and eventually melodic instruments as the boys expressed serious interest in learning to play.

Radio and television programs were carefully evaluated in family discussion, often quite heated discussion. Gradually only worthwhile and interesting programs were selected. Frequently, by choice, reading or quiet study replaced passive listening and viewing. In all family discussions, the parents emphasized the importance of speaking clearly and being proud of having something interesting to talk about. The parents provided the best speech and conversation of which they were capable to serve as models for the boys.

After the meeting many parents gathered around the woman who had shared her experience so freely to thank her and tell her that she had been an inspiration to them. No one could doubt that education of high quality for that family was not limited to the hours the children spent in school but went on every waking hour in a home that by economic standards might have been classified as disadvantaged.

It seems unnecessary to say that these boys did exceedingly well in their school work and were leaders in playground activities. With their father and mother continuously concerned about improving themselves through learning, the children could hardly escape believing that learning is one of the most valuable and delightful activities in life and that schools are the gateway to deep and meaningful learning.

Innovations in Meeting Educational Needs

Homes will not be good places for children unless their parents live satisfying, self-fulfilling lives. Teachers of middle-class background have no basis in experience, and, therefore are truly unable, even in imagination, to conjure up a vision of what dire poverty means in the daily living of men and women not greatly unlike themselves.

The comfort, convenience and beauty of a middle-class home is sometimes taken for granted if the teacher has had no other experience. Frequently these favorable conditions actually stimulate other materialistic desires and people work to provide themselves with a swimming pool, a more elaborately decorated and furnished home, or seasonal perfection in landscaping their gardens. No one could take exception to these dreams and aspirations. But with such promises at the end of the rainbow, many people are truly too preoccupied to be sensitive to the bleak existences that many of their neighbors live.

The leadership in the schools of a small city (Tulare, California) knew that many of the children and families they served were in deep trouble. The superintendent, Max Cochrane, sought help for them long before the Economic Opportunity Act of 1964 and the Elementary and Secondary Education Act of 1965 were passed by Congress. The work of the Assistant Superintendent, Mrs. Thelma Gomez, brought her into daily contact with disadvantaged children. She called them "Thursday's children" because they "had far to go." For two years the city schools operated a preschool project for three-, four- and five-year-olds. It was generously funded by the Rosenberg Foundation. This project operated from 1964–1966 as a research study to determine the effectiveness of certain procedures in facilitating language, social, and cognitive development of children from a disadvantaged milieu, which was also culturally different. The project which served 26 children terminated in June 1966 and the research became the basis of a doctoral study.[6]

Bilingual aides from the community were employed and trained in the Preschool Project. They assisted in communicating with the parents of Mexican background who came to the school as frequent and welcome visitors. The aides also became valuable interpreters of the purposes of the program to parents whose children were not actually involved in the project and other people in the community. These aides from the community were able to talk to many people whom the school is not always able to reach. People who have not been well treated are likely to be suspicious, but they have confidence in the aides from their own group who convince them that teachers are dedicated people.

Having the teacher aides gave the children more opportunity to work with adults who understood and liked them. One aide reported on the degree of rapport she finally established with one of the children. The colorful toys of the nursery school had a fatal attraction for Juan whose suspiciously bulging pockets were inspected and unloaded as the children got ready to board the bus at the close of the session. Finally the aide was able to help him understand that the toys were for all the children to play with but could be borrowed, now and then, to play with at home. "Oh, I see," said Juan, "no stealing without asking!"

These children were able to build a good image of themselves; they were not afraid to try new experiences; they grew rapidly in the social graces imitative of the adults who treated them so warmly and understandingly. These non-English speaking children are caught in a cross-cultural conflict and special intervention is needed if they are not to be cut off from the mainstream of our culture.

The aides themselves grew in sensitivity to the children. A child who had been one of the most lively in the group arrived one morning as quiet as if he were almost stunned. When the opportunity came to talk

[6] Armistre Ametjian, *The Effect of a Preschool Program Upon the Intellectual Development and Social Competency of Lower Class Children,* Stanford University, 1966.

to the teacher in charge, the aide asked: "What could have happened
to a child to take all the pep and enthusiasm out of him?"

The overcrowded homes of many disadvantaged children afford them
no quiet place for study or reading. On the recommendation of the school
authorities, the Tulare City Inter-Racial Council, made up of representatives of various governmental, civic, religious, public and private agencies,
has for several years operated a study center four nights each week. It
provides young people in grades 7–14 a place to study with a professionally trained teacher to assist and with appropriate reference and
library material available. The effect on the life of the family as well as
the improved educational achievement of the students was quickly noted.
Every evening an average of 35 students made use of the facilities at the
Lincoln School, where 90 percent of the regular enrollment comes from
minority groups.

As federal funds became available to this district, a Head Start program
based on the rich experience gained in the Preschool Project was launched
with a minimum of difficulty, and plans were made to provide compensa-
tory educational experiences for disadvantaged school age children during
the summer session and the regular school term.

Excellent objectives for the entire program were carefully formulated.
One purpose that was particularly emphasized predicts a more understanding and humane relationship between home and school. The school
authorities proposed "to maintain home-school environmental relationships in which each agency supports the other and where cultural expectations and practices do not create unduly great or burdensome con-
flicts."

The Tulare school people recognized that

> An important need of many children who live in subcultures
> which are significantly different from the prevailing culture relates
> to finding ways whereby cultural conflicts can be modified or
> lessened. To the extent that the mores and expectations of the
> home are at cross-purposes with the expectations and standards
> of the school, serious conflicts and frustrations may result for
> children who too often become unwitting victims of such situa-
> tions. They need to have home-school relationships which will
> assist their parents in more effectively supporting the educational
> efforts of the school and which will help the school recognize the
> realities of their subcultures and assist by helping families modify
> that subculture when change is indicated, and accept its realities

in terms of educational planning if those realities cannot or should not be modified.

This statement of belief represents a long step in intercultural understanding. The complete realization of this purpose will take a long time but the position stated will give direction to the efforts of parents and teachers.

The Tulare school people committed themselves to providing many direct, firsthand experiences to contribute to the children's cognitive development and to give deeper meaning to, and stimulate greater interest in, more abstract aspects of learning. In this connection, they said:

> One of the most important needs of disadvantaged children relates to their relative lack of opportunities to have many experiences such as travel, being introduced to many and interesting people outside of their own subcultures, observing and learning about many scientific phenomena, becoming aware of many historical and cultural aspects of human experience, and, in general, to acquire a rich and varied experiential background which will enable them to react with understanding, realism and interest to the more abstract curriculum of the school. They cannot read with meaning or understanding about topics which are completely unknown to them; they cannot be expected to write either informatively or creatively if they have had few significant or stimulating experiences to write about; they cannot be expected to create that which is beautiful or significant unless they have had at some time experiences in observing or sensing that which is beautiful; they cannot be expected to become skillful in problem solving unless they have actual experiences in analyzing and struggling with real problems.

As the staff worked consciously with parents to achieve intercultural understanding and mutual acceptance and as they undertook to broaden the horizons of children through providing firsthand enriching experiences, they found themselves confronted by a problem of which they were not previously aware. Although the children's background of experience was meager, it was only slightly less meager than that of their parents. And so, reasoned the staff, the opportunity for firsthand experiences must be made available to the parents as well as the children in order not to increase the social distance between them. The staff set itself the question: Should we encourage parents to go on the study trips planned for the children? The staff agreed that the trips would serve

1. To provide many rich experiences related to the major culture
2. To establish school-family relationships which are mutually supportive
3. To help the family become aware of resources related to the health, welfare and education of their children
4. To assist families to understand their children better, to accept the realities of their strengths and weaknesses, and to become aware of how they grow, develop, and learn
5. To help families to participate in relationships which would enhance and improve their self-esteem.

Two kinds of trips were provided, one-day trips for parents and children and weekend trips for entire families.

The one-day trips were planned to provide experiences of a cultural enrichment nature and to provide opportunities for parents and children to share new interests and new cultural experiences. These trips included visits to Lincoln Preschool, Self-Help Housing Development, Fresno Mall and Train Ride, Bakersfield Historical Museum, Fresno Zoo, Bakersfield Airport, Art Gallery and Courthouse, San Miguel Mission and others.

The Tulare District has participated with other districts in the planning and implementation of a program of outdoor education which is known locally as *Scicon* and which provides for a week's experience in outdoor education and living in the high Sierra for all sixth-grade children. The emphasis is upon science and conservation education and social development. The opportunities for intergroup relationships are considered an especially valuable component of this program which is funded by the Tulare County Board of Education, by the participating districts and by private contributions.

Three of the weekend trips for family groups were made to *Scicon*. One was made to the coast near Hearst's Castle. The weekend trips were arranged so that families could spend two days and two nights together in new and interesting environments. In the mountains the groups went on nature walks, listened to talks by forest rangers, enjoyed games, camp fire programs, viewed films and heard about the science and conservation education programs in which their children were participating.

The trip to the coast included an exploration of the beach and visits to the state park and fishing port. It provided an opportunity for the majority of these families to stay in a motel for the first time, dine at a large restaurant, and see the ocean and the beach. For many of them this was the longest trip they had ever taken and the first time they had ever been away from home.

Following the trips, the adults were asked to write what they thought about these experiences if they wished to. Many of the evaluations were written in Spanish. All were most interesting but a few quotations will supply the general reaction and show what these experiences meant to the participating mothers and fathers:

> "This place made me feel young again . . ."
>
> "Thank you for making it possible for mothers to go on this trip and to rest from work and worrying about bills . . ."
>
> "The trip was a change from the everyday routine. I'm sure the kids enjoyed themselves, with all the area to play in, and I really enjoyed myself, too."
>
> "I've never had a chance to go anywhere like this before and don't guess I ever will again . . ."
>
> "It was wonderful to see the joy in our children's faces as they played in the beautiful outdoors, as they ate so heartily and looked forward to all the plans you made for us."
>
> "This trip has been the most fun my family (four children) has ever had . . ."
>
> "This trip was the first one we ever made . . . everything was exciting for us."
>
> "The kids really enjoyed the beach for they had never been to one."
>
> "We talk about nothing else since we came home except what we saw on the trip."
>
> "We never had much to talk about with the children but now everyone wants to tell about what he liked most . . ."
>
> "The trips on Thursday make it a special day for me to look forward to. I think I am nicer around the house to my husband and to my children because I am always planning for next Thursday."

An important outcome of this effort was the self-esteem built in children and their parents. If a teacher thinks that certain children will do less well than other children because of their ethnic origin, family background, language deficiency or the scores they obtain on intelligence tests (which may be wholly inappropriate to their experiential background), the children will live up to this expectation. This is one way the self-fulfilling prophecy works.

These school people demonstrated both by their words and by their actions that they liked these children, that they enjoyed knowing their parents, that they wanted to share interesting experiences with them, that they were eager to put forth personal effort for them, that they accepted them as friends, that they really cared. Persons so treated live up to what they can be. The self-fulfilling prophecy works this way too.

Teachers must become involved with the people in the community. Too frequently we absolve ourselves from responsibility by enumerating the causes of their troubles. We say, "the families are too large," "their income is too low," "they lack regular employment," "parents are irresponsible," "they don't know how to take care of their money." All these may be included in the causes, but for each problem we have the resources to find a solution. Blaming people for the conditions they find themselves in renders us less able to apply the remedies which are at hand to raise their standard of living. No one wants to be poor or ill or rejected. And no one needs to be if our commitment in this county to democratic principles and ideals is genuine.

Chapter Nine

DEVELOPING
PROGRAM
INNOVATIONS_____

In a democracy, whenever innovations in school programs are to be developed, the school system is dependent upon the goodwill of the parents. Only if the school system maintains the confidence of parents will it be able to function effectively. When a school system needs to keep pace with the times by modifying the curriculum, the school system must work closely with parents in order to retain their steadfast belief that the schools are providing a good education for their children.

Whenever educators are convinced that an entirely new curriculum or some basic curriculum changes should be incorporated in the current school program, they take the initiative in explaining to parents and others in the community the nature of the improvement. New courses in foreign language, mathematics, science and reading are being developed in elementary schools. At meetings of parents and teachers, talks and exhibits by school people help parents understand what is underway. Teachers are prepared not only to teach the children the new studies, but also to explain their worth to parents. Adult education programs offer courses in new mathematics and foreign languages which enable middle-class parents to prepare themselves for helping their sons and daughters understand the value of new courses. Periodicals and newspapers report on progress in the development of the new programs and thus encourage people in accepting and appreciating their value.

Since children are the "consumers" of any new school program, parents are concerned that their children are receiving an education of excellent quality and are being well prepared for living a good life. Parents need to be reassured that their children are receiving as good an education as their parents did.

Parents know the worth of their own education and, unless they learn the worth of newer developments, they are apt to expect the familiar educational patterns to continue. In fact, their faith in the schools depends upon their ability to relate their educational experience to that of their children. They can have faith if the schools take time to explain the changes and the reasons for making them.

Failure to give attention to parental and community confidence can become expensive in terms of tax support, administrative turnover, and successful teaching-learning situations for children. Parental understanding of new school programs must not be left to chance. When curricular innovations are considered, the first step is to plan both parent and teacher involvement in their development. Teacher involvement is the guarantee that the innovation will be successfully launched in the classrooms; parent involvement is the guarantee that the innovation will have wholehearted support from the board of trustees and the local community.

In their role as citizens, parents as well as others in the community are concerned that new programs in the school are developed carefully and responsibly. They want to be sure that the tax dollars which go to education are spent to the best possible advantage. The parents are concerned that the schools maintain worthwhile elements of their operation and that they continuously strive to improve it. This basic responsibility of parents must be recognized by the schools, and plans for improvement and innovation must take parental responsibility into account.

Steps in Improvement and Innovation

As schools and parents work together, they will consider several basic questions, including the following:

> What changes do we expect to take place in our children as a result of their attendance at elementary school?

> What are the really basic needs of children, and to what extent are our schools meeting them? (a) Are there needs which appear critical at this time? (b) Are there needs which educators are especially aware of now? (c) Have there been

changes in numbers of pupils or in the style of life from which they came? Do these influence the needs of children to be met through the school?

What can the schools do which they are not now doing? (a) Are improvements possible? (b) Are they feasible?

Where do we start? What are the steps to be taken? At what points shall we evaluate progress and reconsider plans?

Such assessment of children's needs as a basis for planning school improvements will remind many parents of the market research that they do in business. Indeed, it is just exactly that. The schools are one of the largest businesses in the nation, and they do well to use the techniques which modern business finds esential to survival. Market research emphasizes the importance of knowing facts—hard data—also of knowing consumer opinions, opinions of consumers representing each style of life, opinions of consumers in each age bracket, opinions of consumers of varying amounts of experience and ability. Similarly elementary schools need to have hard data and to know the opinions of the parents in their community, especially their expectations of what the schools should do and their sense of responsibility about what they are to do as parents.

When school and parents are working together to develop readiness for some school improvement, the school makes use of whatever hard data it has on hand. What products of the school program can be displayed as evidence of pupil achievement? What data can be reported in the press and on the public platform about what local pupils have done on standardized tests of achievement? What outstanding pupils can be interviewed and photographed with completed work or work in progress for newspaper releases? Such factual evidence of accomplishment is convincing.

Everyone concerned should know the current status of a school program as a basis for assessing its success and the need for improvements in it. To assess the need for improvements requires a careful look at the goal to be achieved. What changes in the behavior of pupils are to be expected as a consequence of the program? What is the evidence that each of these goals is being attained—in part or entirely? In terms of goal achievement and program participants, administrators and public can take satisfaction in the program. In these instances in which expected goals were not reached, changes are needed in the program, or goals need to be redefined more realistically.

Gaining Parent Acceptance for New Programs

Parents are so important in the functioning of schools that their understanding of school innovations cannot be taken for granted. When the school administrators determine the need for curriculum improvement, they need to have parent communication channels functioning smoothly. With leading parents as members of the parent-teacher association, the school has easy access to key parents in the community. Many a curriculum improvement was initially explored at a meeting attended by parents. The account of the meeting in the local newspaper brought it to the attention of other parents and members of the community.

School administrators need to communicate early with the quiet, long-time residents, who consider earnestly what is best for the community. The people who are looked to as community leaders are then able to reassure their friends that what the school is doing is in the best interests of the community. Understanding on the part of community leaders is one of the best guarantees that the community will have confidence in school innovations and their eventual effects on all of the school children.

Often the school has an advisory committee of outstanding leaders among parents and other citizens in the community. Such an advisory committee is large enough to be representative of the points of view prevalent in the community, but also small enough for members to sit around a table for a discussion. With such a group, school leaders bring up arguments for and against the proposed innovation and guide the group discussion in developing a framework of thought which will support the proposed innovation. The deliberations of the small advisory committee provide a pilot study for the subsequent general meeting attended by parents.

When a parent-teacher association is operating smoothly, curriculum improvements are easily introduced to the community through regular meetings of the association. For instance, a parent-teacher arrangement to capitalize on Public Schools Week will include plans for telling about curriculum innovations. The general meeting of parents will include a talk that describes each innovation as a means for improving the current curriculum offering and helping boys and girls advance successfully in their studies. The individual conferences between parents and teachers in the classrooms will include mention of the innovation and how it will affect the children selected with the consent of their parents to participate in the pilot program. Room displays and general displays in the auditorium will further explain the innovation and its eventual effect on all of the school children.

A "letter to parents" can be used effectively to make Public Schools Week a setting for public relations and development of community understanding of curriculum innovations. Here is an example of such a letter that helped to further community understanding and appreciation of new school programs in character education, in mathematics and on-going programs in music, student government, literature, and after school recreation.

UNIFIED SCHOOL DISTRICT
SUBURBIA ELEMENTARY SCHOOL
PUBLIC SCHOOLS WEEK BULLETIN TO PARENTS

April 19

Dear Parents:

We cordially invite you to our annual observance of Public Schools Week at Suburbia School.

You will be receiving a special invitation to visit your child's room. In addition, you may be interested in visiting some of the following special classes:

Student Council Committee	8:30 A.M. Monday	Auditorium
Special Literature	9:00 A.M. Monday	Library
Orchestra	8:30 A.M. Tuesday	Auditorium
Instrument classes	Tuesday	Auditorium
Speech	Daily	Rooms 3 and 8
Glee Club	8:30 A.M. Friday	Auditorium

Open House will be held on *Tuesday, April 2, from 7:00 to 9:00 P.M.* All classrooms will be open to parents, children, and friends who do not have children in school. Pupils should act as guides for their parents, and should show their folders of school work to them.

Each classroom will have room mothers as hostesses to see that all visitors meet the teacher. Parents can arrange individual conferences with the teacher for a later date.

P.T.A. MEETING. As an introduction to Open House, our Parent-Teacher Association is planning a welcome at 6:45 P.M. in the Auditorium. Our school orchestra will give a brief concert. Please come early for this special treat.

Special Exhibits to see Tuesday night include the following:

a. Award-winning children's books on display in the library.
b. Character Education exhibit in the Cafeteria.
c. After-school and summer playground exhibit in Cafeteria.
d. Audio-visual materials in the library.
e. Modern mathematics materials in the Auditorium.

"Help Build America—Support Our Public Schools" is the theme of our Public Schools Week this year. We hope you will all find time to visit schools sometime during the week.

Cordially yours,

Principal
Suburbia School

Developing New Programs

Dr. Lawrence Borosage,[1] in talking at a National Leadership Seminar, brought out several points about program development that pertain to program innovation in the elementary school. He enumerates a variety of capabilities important in those who take responsibility for developing and improving programs as follows:

1. . . . the capacity and the willingness to see the community and its . . . education needs as a whole rather than a collection of agencies and self-interests. . . .

2. . . . the capacity to set some common goals, to fix priorities, to develop new approaches, to test these in action and to evaluate performance against national as well as local standards. . . .

3. . . . the capacity to mobilize governmental as well as private resources and to forge working relationships among agencies of both sectors. . . .

[1] Lawrence Borosage, "A Framework for Program Development," *A National Leadership Seminar on Home Economics Education.* Columbus, Ohio: The Center for Vocational and Technical Education, 1966, pp. 29–45.

4. The capacity to involve and to affect critical centers of community power. . . .

5. The capacity to finance the considerable cost of research and experimentation. . . .

6. . . . the capacity to convince the people involved . . . that these programs are for real; they are not window dressings for the *status quo,* not a crumb dropped conspicuously by the affluent few who dine at the community main table.

Dr. Borosage also enumerates thirteen "leadership sensitivities" as follows:

Communication

We must consider communication as it relates to the other twelve leadership sensitivities. . . .

Ends

Anyone in the leadership capacity must have the ability to do two kinds of things concerning the ends of the program. One is to state the objectives very clearly. . . .
. . . in addition to the specific objectives, we also must consider longe-range goals. . . . one leadership sensitivity is to try to answer the question: What are we about or what are we trying to do?

Means

How are we going to try to achieve the objective or how are we going to try to achieve the goals which we have established for ourselves? What kinds of plans are we going to develop? What kind of long-range plan will expedite the long-range goal? What kind of planning is needed for short-range goals? Of more importance, how will we link the long-range and the short-range goals?

Role Identification

. . . Who is going to be responsible for what? For example, what is the role of the advisory committee? Can we define the role of that committee clearly? Will that committee see itself as a policy-making body rather than an advisory body? In the past, when advisory committees have gotten into difficulty, it was frequently because their roles had not been clearly defined. . . .

Atmosphere

The next leadership sensitivity . . . is creating the kind of an atmosphere in which people can work together . . . the feeling, the tone, or the mood that exists in a group of people who are attempting to work together to arrive at some common goals. . . .

Participation

We are talking about more than just merely getting people together to sit down and talk about some of our problems. There are three ideas in this matter of participation. . . . First . . . , it is the mental and emotional involvement of people. People who are really going to participate in program development—"I am really in on this thing." Second, to gain effective participation the individuals must feel that somehow they are making a contribution to the situation. Third, they must sense a responsibility for sharing.

Identity

Identity is a leadership sensitivity that may be a problem. We have found community and agency people are willing to come together; they are willing to discuss a problem; they may be willing to say, "Yes, we will cooperate in the solution of the problem." Then everyone leaves and nothing much happens. . . . Part of the problem is that people want identity; they want to sense some identification. . . . When these people begin to feel that they are losing their identity and are being subordinated to something else, watch and see what happens. They are not going to be interested in having a part in what we are attempting to achieve.

Individual Differences

Sensitivity to individual differences among the agencies with which we work cannot be overlooked. Their objectives and their goals may not be the same as those that you cherish. Consequently, we must recognize that there are differences in the groups as well as the people with whom we will be working.

Social Control

When we get groups of people to work together we find that in reality there are two types of organizations at work—formal and informal. The formal organization may be reflected in a kind of organizational chart. . . . In program development we need to recognize the way activities take place may not be indicated in the organizational pattern; this is largely because of the informal interaction that takes place among people.

Human Relations

Sensitivity to human relations would seem to be self-explanatory. . . .

Group Standards

The standards of the group influence the criteria for the program.

Group Evaluation

If we have established certain kinds of goals and objectives, we need to ask periodically, "How are we doing?"

Size

We are going to have to recognize when we talk about the concepts of size, and communication and programs that what is done in a smaller community is, of necessity, different from that which is done in a large community. . . .

Curricular Areas for School-Parent Innovation

In general, it is essential that school and home cooperate regarding school matters close to areas in which parents feel responsibility and express concern. For instance, the school that serves a less advantaged community is apt to have incident after incident in which parents express their concern that children return home after school safely. Noting the frequency of such incidents, the school will work with parents in developing its after-school activities for the children, and will make a point of including provisions for participating children to go home without danger of being molested on the way.

Although the school needs to work with its parents whenever it is developing a curricular innovation, it is especially important for the school and parents to work closely together on such matters as preschool programs and sex education units.

Preschool programs: In every community, the school receives children from their parents at the time of beginning school. If the school begins with the first grade, then parents of six-year-old children bring them to the school and entrust the children to the teacher for part of the day. If the school begins with nursery school or kindergarten, then parents of children of an age appropriate for entry bring their children to have the teacher take responsibility for their learning activities during the hours in school.[2]

Parental interest and concern is not cut off abruptly the first day of school. The fact that they continue is readily seen in the numbers of parents who come to school when the school holds open house for parents and others in the community. Parent attendance is highest in the preschool rooms, next highest in the first grade rooms, and diminishes in subsequent grade rooms.

The school will do well to work with parents as soon as they bring their children to enroll them in school, and to continue working with them from that point on. To do this successfully, school people need to think carefully about the preschool program. They must note the nature of the community and assess the needs of its preschool children. School personnel inform themselves about the nature of preschool children at each age level and think which program is most appropriate to further development of each child. This process of a school orienting itself is the first step in its working cooperatively with parents in developing the preschool program. The process is described here in terms of an individual school.

Excelsior City served its elementary school population in fourteen separate elementary schools in a community located about thirty miles from a large metropolitan center. Fathers and mothers of the children in school were employed in the usual variety of occupations found in such a community. Some parents commuted daily to professional, executive, business, and technical employment in the nearby city; others found comparable employment locally. Because Excelsior City was located on a main highway leading to a large population center, employment in motels, restaurants, garages, and service stations exceeded that which might have been expected in other communities of comparable size. Excelsior City was also the center of a farming area in which seasonal agricultural labor was employed at various seasons to plant, cultivate, and harvest crops.

The community was reasonably prosperous with only a few families in an exceedingly advantaged position. About 25 percent of the families were definitely socioeconomically disadvantaged, especially those in which the breadwinner had no technical skills and depended upon the demand for agricultural labor locally or in more distant agricultural

[2] Vivian Edmiston Todd and Helen Heffernan, *The Years Before School—Guiding Preschool Children.* New York: The Macmillan Company, 1964.

areas of the region. Most of these workers were of Mexican background. Although many of the men spoke English, Spanish was generally spoken in the homes and the children entered school completely without command of English, the language in which instruction was given. A rapidly growing Negro population was increasing the competition for jobs available to unskilled male workers. Little domestic employment was available for Negro women.

After government funds became available for preschool groups, the success of a Head Start program begun in 1965 was most gratifying to the school administrators. Children below kindergarten age gave evidence of improved health, good physical development, a happy acceptance of the new environment, increased language facility, and an insatiable curiosity and tireless energy in exploring and interacting with the stimulating outdoor and indoor environment provided for them. The enthusiasm of the director and the professional staff was reflected in the high morale of the aides, who were drawn from the deprived segment of the community, and in the often expressed appreciation of the parents who visited the center as frequently as their employment permitted. They came and talked with the teachers directly or through one of the aides who served as interpreter for the non-English speaking parents.

In the fourteen elementary schools, kindergarten teachers were employed, each serving two groups of kindergarten children of approximately thirty each in two sessions of 150 minutes. The administration in Excelsior City had long been concerned about the educational program in the kindergarten and was acutely aware of the overcrowded conditions as a constant threat to the development of young people. Under the tension created by the situation, children were rushed through and regimented in activities. Much of the program was artificial and contrived to keep the children quiet. The large groups and the short session made it difficult to arrange any direct, meaningful, firsthand experiences. Although the administrators in charge had long envisioned a kindergarten program in which parent participation would be of the utmost value, they recognized that to ask kindergarten teachers to relate themselves in any significant way to 120 parents was ridiculous.

The administrators concluded that the conditions under which kindergartens were operating undermine interest, destroy zest, and actually lay a foundation for later apathy toward school, failure, alienation, or rebellion. Although the administrative personnel had long been committed to an educational philosophy of maximum, harmonious development of a child's powers—physically, intellectually, socially, and emotion-ally—they were forced to admit that existing conditions in the kinder-garten were not conducive to the development of imagination, creativity, sensitivity, flexibility, and curiosity.

The administrators had also long been concerned about the educa-tional program particularly in the first grade and in the subsequent primary grades.

Every first-grade teacher carried on her activities as though teaching six-year-olds to read was her major responsibility. This attitude on the part of teachers was no doubt due to the pressure they felt because Excelsior School is located in a state that has adopted a statewide testing program in reading. The testing program puts pressure on administrators to have the district "make a good showing." Teachers, likewise, are fully conscious of this pressure and inevitably put pressure on children "to have our class show up well on the state tests."

The mental health of the child seems of less importance than meeting these adult expectancies whether they come from the state or the local community. That many children are not physically, neurologically, or experientially ready to read at six has been demonstrated again and again by specialists in vision, neurology, psychology, and education. Although first-grade teachers can recite the needs of the young child as a result of their professional training, they feel under pressure to drive all six-year-olds down standardized roads to reading. They say "the law de-mands it" and "the community demands it." But neither the law nor the most vociferous community demand will make a child walk before he is ready, talk before he is ready, or cause his teeth to erupt before he has reached the proper maturation level. Neither will any law or community demand produce magic which will make it possible for even the best qualified teacher to connect in children's minds the visual symbol and its meaning until the growth of the sheathing on the frontal lobes of the brain is complete. About 25 percent of our children will probably be unable to complete successfully the present reading expectancies of the traditional first-grade program. Actually our present overexpectations are nullifying or even destroying the best in many children.

This, then, was the complex problem as the Excelsior City adminis-trators saw it. This is a problem so general in the United States and so generally accepted that the spread of misconceptions has achieved epidemic proportions. School administrators either refuse to look at the problem hoping it will go away, or seek hither and thither for panaceas that they can see in advance will not solve the real problem.

They raise all kinds of questions:

1. Can children learn as rapidly as adults would like them to by grouping them into bright, average and slow groups? No evidence exists in the professional literature that any kind of homogeneous grouping results in greater academic achievement. The deleterious effect on the child's self-concept would cause any conscientious educator to hesitate about attempting to solve the problem by this method.

2. Should some children be retained in kindergarten if they are not ready for first grade? This question implies a prescribed grade standard which every child must attain regardless of the individual variations in ability, physical equipment, experience background, and the like. Research indicates that retention usually has a discouraging effect on the child which results in less effort and may lead the child to believe that he is a failure.

3. Should we set up a two-year kindergarten for the socio-economically disadvantaged? Some countries provide a two-year kindergarten which delays entrance into first grade and lessens the danger of pressure on children for learning to read. A well designed kindergarten program will develop children's concepts which are basic to success in reading far more than the present emphasis on acquiring the skill of reading in a first grade.

4. Should we establish a "pre-first grade?" A "pre-first grade" conveys to parents that their children are not bright enough to enter a regular first grade and make a successful adjustment to it. The experience of thoroughly qualified educators who have tested this type of organization has led them eventually to discard it because of the low expectancies teachers had for the children and because of the poor public relations it caused,

There is no easy solution to the problem. School people—teachers and administrators alike—should overcome any urge to be omnipotent, or any need to manipulate, to manage, or to plan the lives of others. We should give all children freedom to grow and develop according to their own individual inner timetable. The teacher's role is not one of imposing the same set of standards on every child, but rather to help each child to take his next developmental step in attaining expectations established for him in the light of his potential.

The problem faced by Excelsior City and thousands of other schools calls for new thinking, new approaches, and new attitudes. This is precisely the kind of problem which cannot be solved by school people alone. It will certainly never be solved by administrative tinkering, community edicts, or rigid adherence to curricular standards, an adherence detrimental to the self-confidence of children.

The problem poses many tasks for leadership which include:

1. Working with lay and professional organizations so that local representatives to the state legislature will have authoritative information on problems of individual differences among children and groups of children served by the schools, of the flexible adaptation of instruction required to meet these needs, and of the dangers to mental development caused by excessive pressure on children.

2. Helping parents and the public in general to understand the facts, to act resolutely in terms of them, and have courage to take a realistic approach to needed change from traditional practice.

3. Correcting the intolerable 60 to 1 pupil-teacher ratio by providing single-session kindergartens enrolling a maximum of 25 children and defining the functions of the kindergarten teacher with regard to relationships with parents and the successful induction of children into the elementary school program.

4. Providing a teachable-size class in grades one, two, and three; assigning a maximum of 25 children per teacher.

5. Providing in-service education for primary teachers to define and identify the needs of young children and learn

to develop programs that will meet adequately individual needs.

6. Developing sales resistance to gadget salesmen who have a commercial interest in selling "sure-cure" ways of further-ing child development toward adult goals by the expendi-ture of public funds on too frequently worthless material.

Sex education: Another area in which curricular innovations are of high concern to parents is that of sex education.[3]

Every spring in middle-class communities across the nation, common talk deals with the local school girl pregnancy. The boys at the paper corner ask each other, "Who is the father?" The girls who knew her in class wonder what she will do. The women of the community discuss the role that the girl's mother played, or did not play, in the affair. The girl and members of her family find themselves caught up in emotion-ally charged scenes as they come to grips with behavior contrary to the mores of their style of life.

Often the mother of the pregnant girl tries to exonerate herself in some way. Desperate about her own reputation as well as that of her daughter, she may attempt to retain some community respect by getting blame shouldered on someone else, or at least by getting someone to share her misery. Teachers and school administrators who were sympa-thetic or made helpful suggestions have been known to lose their jobs at the insistence of an irate mother with no evidence of their involve-ment except the accusation made by the pregnant daughter or imagined by herself.

The personal tragedies of school-age pregnancies can be lessened by provision in the school curriculum for family life education, including sex education at appropriate points. Parents do the best that they can in educating their children but the large numbers of unmarried mothers at young ages is evidence that parents need help with sex education. Parent education programs, together with family life education units for upper grade children in the elementary school, help young people obtain information and develop much needed attitudes.[4]

3 Neil Ulman. "The Facts of Life: More Schools Introduce Sex Education Courses— Often Aiming at Very Young," *The Wall Street Journal,* September 19, 1967.
4 Helen Manley, *Family Life and Sex Education in the Elementary School.* Washing-ton, D.C.: Department of Elementary-Kindergarten-Nursery Education, National Education Association,

On August 30, 1966 the United States Commissioner of Education, Harold Howe II, issued an official policy on family life and sex education as follows:

> The United States Office of Education takes the position that each community and educational institution must determine the role it should play in the area of family life education and sex education; that only the community and its agencies and institutions can know what is desirable, what is possible, and what is wise for them in this role.
>
> To assist communities and educational institutions which wish to initiate or improve programs in this area, the Office of Education will support family life education and sex education as an integral part of the curriculum from preschool to college and adult levels; it will support training for teachers and health and guidance personnel at all levels of instruction; it will aid programs designed to help parents carry out their roles in family life education and sex education; and it will support research and development in all aspects of family life education and sex education.
>
> The Office will work closely with other agencies, both Federal and State, to insure the most effective use of our resources in the implementation of this policy.

The Superintendent of Lebanon Public Schools[5] has described how he and his staff have developed sex education in the junior high school. Prospective teachers of the course, nurse, psychologist, guidance counselors, principal, and superintendent worked together in developing instruction plans. These plans were presented to the Board of Education with the recommendation that such a course be approved. It was.

Further work with parents in developing a ninth grade health unit on sex education is described as follows:

> Our next step was an exchange of ideas with the parents of our ninth grade students. The state consultant served as the leader for this parent conference. Through this meeting, parents became better acquainted with the need for the program, its objectives and the contents of the course of study. The leader conducted a question and answer period. Parents came for information and were not skeptical or antagonistic.

[5] George A. Hartman, "Family Life and Sex Education in the Junior High Schools," *Ohio's Health,* 19: 26–28, (March, 1967).

Books on sex education were loaned to parents. Several excellent films were shown which gave parents a deeper insight into the nature of the subject. Parents were kept informed on the regular class discussions. They were not critical; they were there because of a real interest in the subject. We devoted considerable effort in establishing instruction that would not embarrass anyone. We made parents truly welcome and the relationship helped develop our unit on sex education without criticism.

Announcements were sent home and any parents who objected were allowed to withdraw their child. Last year, we had a few students who did not participate. This year the course is so successfully established that we met little resistance to class attendance. Those excused from the unit on sex education were given special health assignments so that they suffered no loss of credit in health.

With dating, going steady, and getting married occurring at increasingly early ages, it is important for school and parents to work together for the welfare of young people and the social order. Sexual fertility often precedes willingness and ability to take responsibility for caring for children. Society should have young couples who know their roles as parents and are willing to make decisions in terms of the good of their children rather than their own momentary desires.

Both teachers and parents of young adolescents will find it advantageous to consider together the educational implications of such circumstances as the following:

- Most girls who drop out of high school do so in order to marry.
- Effective birth control methods are readily available.
- Young people generally are not aware of the conditions under which sexual activity is a crime punishable by law.
- In many cases legal responsibility for child support is not understood by young parents.
- Social practices governing relationships between young men and women differ from one style of life to another.

School responsibility for family life education was recognized in 1960 by the White House Conference on Children and Youth when it recommended that "family life courses, including preparation of marriage and parenthood, be instituted as an integral and major part of public education from elementary school through high school." This responsibility in no way interferes with parental responsibility, but is supplementary to it and reinforces what parents do. Furthermore, the responsibility of the school should take into account the responsibility of such other community agencies as the churches and synagogues, parent-teacher associations, and well-baby clinics.

Since 1941 when the American Association of School Administrators recommended the inclusion of sex education in the curriculum, various schools have developed education programs suitable to their communities. These are useful to committees of school and community personnel in planning and developing curricular materials for their own schools. Whatever is developed should be agreeable to both parents and teachers.

Limits of Parent Involvement in Schools

Current encouragement of innovation on the part of schools has led to experimentation with greater parent cooperation in school processes. Such cooperation must be in terms of the basic roles of teachers as experts in working with a group of pupils at a certain grade level, and of parents as experts in working with their individual children longitudinally.

The expected result of parent involvement in schools is to benefit the children. If the creation of a parent role supplements that of the teacher, the role should be developed. But if the role created for parents reduces the interaction of teachers and children, the proposed innovation should be carefully examined, and such questions as the following should be asked:

> *Does the proposed parent role enable teachers to teach children more on an individual basis?*
>
> *Does it enable teachers to guide children in extending their use of new ideas and new skills?*
>
> *Does it enable teachers to provide further learning experiences for children with special needs or special abilities?*
>
> *Or is it an attempt to circumvent reducing the size of a teacher's class?*
>
> *Is it an attempt to replace the skillful education guidance of a teacher with custodial child care?*

Does it propose to lessen the importance of a learning activity by having it carried out without adequate supervision?

Questions like these must be raised whenever a proposed innovation may be primarily in terms of "helping teachers" rather than in terms of really helping children. Here are two proposals that contrast focus on adults with focus on children:

Contrasting Proposals for Parent Participation in Playground Supervision

The following teacher-centered and pupil-centered plans for parent participation in playground supervision in lower elementary school grades contrast plans to bolster teaching in oversized classes with plans to meet needs of pupils more completely in small groups.

Proposal by teacher-centered school: Realization that the elementary school teacher has a day of continuous tension relieved only by lunch hour and brief recesses led our school to an exploration of parental help with playground supervision. By employing parents to be on the playground with the children, it is possible to reduce the number of teachers on duty. Parents will come into their responsibility with children by way of briefing sessions in which they learn the playground rules and have opportunity to think through examples of incidents that can occur on the playground.

Usually parents who are interested in supervising playgrounds are basically interested in children. Those who have experienced the orientation sessions and are still eager to help on the playground are also likely to be competent in working with children, and able to improve their ways of doing so under the guidance of the teacher on duty.

Where parents are employed for playground supervision, they not only help pupils during lunch and after-school periods but also may be helpful to them in out-of-school situations. The parent playground assistant is likely to remain in character in community situations in which adults and children interact. For this reason, children benefit from the employment of parents, both directly in the playground situation and indirectly in the community.

Teachers also benefit from having parents employed for playground supervision. For one thing, teachers with high pupil loads have fewer hours on duty with children. For another, teachers have their effective numbers increased by parent aides who endeavor to help children in the ways that school people do. The whole school benefits by having a larger number of adults in the community activity committed to furthering the best interest of school, teachers, and pupils. Furthermore, all of us as taxpayers benefit by having parent-aides employed at rates below those paid teachers.

Proposal by pupil-centered school: Our school realizes the responsibility that it has for teaching city boys and girls who come from less advantaged homes than those in the suburbs. The average family income in our community probably averages about three thousand dollars. Sixty-five percent of our children come from one-parent families.

We have steadily pushed to obtain smaller classes. Our school district has cooperated by reducing the ratio of pupils to teachers. Now, on the basis of their observations of pupils on the playground and in the classroom, our teachers feel that the classroom is under control but that we still have the problem of helping the children learn better ways of playing together outside of class. We can have more play centers on the playground if we can have an adult present to supervise the use of each kind of equipment.

As a faculty, we have worked out with our PTA leaders the enclosed plan for parent participation in playground supervision. Through a survey of parent work schedules and parent interests in working with children, we have a list of parents who will prepare for, and participate in, playground supervision before school, at noon, and after school. We feel that we can develop a program that will replace unstructured pushing and hitting play with organized games appropriate for each grade level, and that better playground activities for the boys and girls will help them in having better learning situations in the classroom. . . .

Parent participation in team teaching: Team teaching in grades seven and eight also needs careful consideration to make sure that it stems from genuine interest in furthering the development of boys and girls rather than from desire to keep down program costs even if optimum learning may be in jeopardy. Any proposal to add parents to a team of teachers should be made only after asking such questions as the following:

Is there any evidence that changes desired in children occur more frequently and in greater quantity when team teaching replaces the usual self-contained classroom?

Are members of the team working for mastery on the part of each pupil, or are they escaping teacher responsibility for individual child learning by distributing it through the team?

Does each team member have regular opportunity to consider feedback obtained from pupils in writing, and to utilize this written feedback in planning for subsequent teaching?

Are team members working with individual pupils, furthering their acquaintance with each of them through feedback from learning situations?

In some instances, team teaching arrangements supplement well qualified teachers with beginning teachers who are also mothers returning to employment after the years in which they bore children and started their development into interesting and self-sufficient persons. Where such parents are part of the teaching team, they bring to it a realistic point of view which is helpful to teachers in planning out-of-school activities and assignments for pupils, and is helpful to pupils who are in need of parental guidance. The counseling dimension of a teaching team can be increased by parents who are combining study of psychology and education with their team participation.

Currently in California an innovative project is exploring the usefulness of parents in supplementing teacher visits to homes of students. Parent members of a team find it easy to learn to communicate with parents of different styles of life as well as parents in circumstances similar to their own. Parents on a team as home visitors can serve as a two-way channel of communication between home and school. At one and the same time they can help parents understand what the school is trying to do, and can help teachers understand what problems pupils and parents face at home. Having a parent on the teacher team may be an important way of lessening the gap between the middle-class teacher and the less advantaged and often fragmented family.

Parent participation in public and private schools: Parent participation in school activities differs according to the style of life of the parents, and according to the nature of the schools. In private schools, parents are encouraged to contribute monetarily in accord with their means; but in public schools, all necessary expenses are paid out of public funds. Thus private schools are associated with families that pride themselves on their educational and other philanthropies, and public schools are associated with families concerned with looking after themselves and paying taxes for what benefits the social order as a whole.

In the rural community in which the public school is more closely associated with welfare agencies than it is in the big cities, the school may have a parent-teacher association which raises funds through an annual community festival—a bazaar, for instance—and uses them subsequently for such philanthropies as providing glasses for the son and daughter of a medically indigent family, or providing the whole community, including the school, with cultural or recreational equipment and programs it might not otherwise have. In these situations, the parents and school personnel operate in their roles as responsible citizens of the community rather than as educators employed by public schools.

In general, if the nation is to have free public education, it must meet needed school expenses out of public funds.

Mental health education for parents: Especially in the school communities of big cities, adult education programs are experimenting with courses for parents ranging from the "New Mathematics" offered in an upper middle-class area to a general offering about how to become more adequate as a parent. A current report by the Board of Education of the City of New York[6] tells about a workshop considering "Mental Health Education for Parents." It recognizes the school as a "natural setting for parent education," and says:

> Parent education uses group discussion to help people examine, clarify, and understand a specific aspect of their life situation— their role as parents. In a group setting and under skilled leadership parents can learn at their own rate, in their own way, and from each other. Learning takes place where there are new insights, new understandings, rather than exposure to intellectual facts. . . . These sessions are used to share opinion and concerns. They are not preplanned, but self-determined. . . . Parent Discussion Group . . . consists of never more than twenty members. The ideal number is fifteen. . . .

[6] Bureau of Child Guidance, Board of Education of the City of New York, *Proceedings of the Bureau of Child Guidance Institute on Mental Health and Education—Realizing the Potential of the Individual in the Great Society.* New York: Bureau of Child Guidance, Board of Education of the City of New York, January, 1966, pp. 363–367.

The content of the parent group discussion is described as follows:

1. Parents should understand the child's needs at every stage. (There is often a wide gap between the facts and parental expectations; the child they have and the type they wanted.)

2. Conscious parental reactions to the child's behavior are explored. The unconscious reactions or the "whys" are not discussed by the group. . . .

3. The leader helps the group to decide the topic area and what part of the topic the group wants to discuss. . . .

4. The leader now works at eliciting a variety of experiences from the members. He broadens the base of the topic by various techniques such as acting as inquirer, playing back, staying with the material.

5. Parents should know that there are a variety of choices of parental reactions in rearing their children.

6. An opportunity to discuss the satisfactions as well as the dissatisfactions in child rearing is an important contribution of the parent discussion groups.[7]

Probably the greatest contribution of adult education classes for parents is to encourage their cooperation with school personnel for the good of their children. As parents understand more fully what the schools are endeavoring to do, they are better able to facilitate and contribute to the educational process.

Administrator X and the Women

Mr. X was a conscientious school administrator who made a point of watching for significant social and educational changes. He had pioneered in introducing the new mathematics into his schools and had gotten the parents in his district as eager for it as his teachers. When foreign language study was emphasized by the National Defense Education Act, he was prepared for expanding the language program at the request of the

[7] *Ibid.,* p. 365.

Parent-Teacher Association because a parent committee of community leaders had been considering the importance of language study.

Now Mr. X was concerned about what was happening to women. His own wife was using her college education as a teacher in an adjoining school district. She had started teaching when their younger child was in school for a full school day. Maybe this was one reason he had been sensitive to the increasing number of articles in magazines and newspapers about working wives. The articles reported that women between the ages of 35 and 54 were in the labor force in large numbers; that most college women are at work except for the few years they use in starting their families; that many wives work part-time and provide supplementary income for helping their sons and daughters in getting an education.

When Mr. X was concerned about a matter, he got the facts about it. He wrote to Women's Bureau in Washington, D.C., and then studied the information booklets that he received. He was especially impressed with the fact that a girl should expect to spend twenty-five or more years in the labor force.

"Are our schools preparing girls for what women are doing in the labor force?" he asked himself. "Women are no longer just a supplement to the labor force; they are an integral part of it. Does what we teach reflect this change?"

Having identified a problem, Mr. X went right to work on it.

He watched for articles interpreting the facts about the employment of women. What were women's magazines saying to women? What were news articles about business and industry saying about women? He was surprised to find that such newspapers as *The Wall Street Journal* were carrying articles about the place of working wives in the urban community, in consumption of services as well as products of industry, and in occupations outside the heavy labor category. He read about the problems and results of enforcing the Civil Rights Act as it pertains to women.

As he read, Mr. X discussed what he read with other responsible people in the community. Now he was surprised at what had been going on "right under his own nose," as he described it. The factory on the far side of the city, he discovered, employed large numbers of women, many of them mothers of school-age children. He began to understand why the parent-teacher meetings after school were not well attended in the schools in that part of the city, and why the parent conferences with teachers at the end of the first grading period had to be scheduled either very early in the morning or in the evening. If mothers and teachers were both working during the day, he thought, the schools had to depend more on telephone conversations and written communications as means for working with parents to help their children.

As the months passed, Mr. X found himself observing more and more practices of the schools that needed to be brought into line with the facts about the working wives of the city. He began to suspect also that each teacher probably would be able to prepare the girls and boys better for the labor force that had evolved, if they started thinking and planning based on the most up-to-date facts.

In the school year of 1966–67, Mr. X was glad to see that the public relations department of the schools was busy with trying to determine what, if anything, was needed in the schools in view of the facts about the employment of women. He could point with satisfaction to the following arrangements:

1. An inspirational address for teachers just before school opened was entitled, "The Myths About Women," and posed the question of whether the schools were preparing girls for the world that teachers knew in their youth or for the world as it really is today.

2. In each of the schools, at least two teachers' meetings were devoted to discussing such topics as "What are women doing these days?" and "How are we preparing girls for employment?"

3. In the program for each of the parent-teacher groups a meeting early in the spring was scheduled around the theme of what the schools are teaching girls and boys about work.

4. With the editor-in-chief of the city paper sympathetic to the need to sensitize the community to the need for curricular changes implicit in the facts about working wives, a reporter was scheduled to be at each important meeting dealing with the topic.

5. An outstanding feature writer for the paper, a woman, was responsible for articles based on materials from the Women's Bureau and census data about the employment of women in the city.

6. In his office files, Mr. X maintained a folder entitled "Citizens Committee on the Status of Women." To this he added names of leading citizens and school people whose public statements showed them to be intelligently informed about the problem, and possible candidates for the committee.

7. Another office folder was receiving articles as they appeared in the local paper, or in periodicals of regional or national scope.

8. Informal conversation before and after meetings of the School Board included discussions of implications of the facts about working wives in general, and about problems of women heads of families in particular.

As Mr. X continued his attempt to identify curricular and administrative changes needed by his school in view of the employment of women, he found like-minded people coming forward to help him. People in leadership positions in education began to understand the handicaps encountered by women heads-of-families since women earn about sixty cents for every dollar earned by a man. They realized the importance of having girls prepare for employment at levels requiring more skills and offering higher remuneration. People in leadership positions in the community realized that the high level of achievement through volunteer activities was furthered by women who had acquired their skills during years of schooling. As they understood more fully the need for education concerning the employment of women, these leaders began to exert their leadership in concurring with the schools in whatever action was needed.

As the efforts of Mr. X were augmented by others, religious services or any other meetings in the city were apt to include talks having some reference to married women as an integral part of the labor force or as skillful workers in the community.

With others carrying more responsibility on public relations, Mr. X turned his attention to technical curriculum and administration matters. The annual schedules of meetings for teachers, parents, and other members of the community are to reflect specific outcomes of the thinking that he and other responsible educators did to improve the school offering.

Mr. X and others in the city schools are reporting to professional groups of educators about the curriculum units developed for social studies, home economics, and business education classes in junior high schools and the new materials for teachers in the upper elementary grades. A research project is underway in the upper grades to determine the proportion of boys and girls who think ahead to having, or being, working wives; and to study what changes, if any, occur in their thinking as they make use of the new curriculum materials.

The counselors and others in the guidance program in the city schools have already developed a collection of booklets about the occupations highly staffed by women. They hope to supplement these by materials written very simply and entertainingly for girls between ten and fifteen years of age to help them think clearly about what a mother does in working outside her home as well as about what a mother does in caring for her children and managing her home. The increased funds for such materials reflect the increased awareness of school and community about the kind of lives girls will be leading when they enter and reenter the labor force in the years ahead.

When the schools begin their unit about occupations and careers, the guidance people and the school librarian display a collection of booklets and books for the children to use. The letter that they send home to parents at that time invites them to make use of the collection also. The parents who do so are those who realize their responsibility for working with the school in guiding their children toward suitable careers.

The schools enhance teacher understanding about the work of the community by having a school day set aside for teachers to visit the businesses and industries of the city. Business and industrial establishments are glad to arrange guided tours for groups of teachers, and to answer their questions about what they see and about company policy in such matters as employment of women. Both business and industry and the teachers of the city believe that the day's program helps the good relation that exists between them, and furthers the preparation of girls and boys for the realities of the labor force.

Teachers in grades five to nine include in social studies a study trip to the nearby Opportunities Industrialization Center. In preparing the class for the visit, the teacher explains the necessity for both men and women to learn new skills when their old job skills are outmoded by technological advance. The eagerness of people to learn what they had no opportunity to learn in childhood is emphasized. "We help ourselves," is the motto of the Center, an important concept for everyone to understand and believe in.

On the study trip the children see how people learn the skills of electronic assembly and inspection, auto repair, typing, machine tool operation, retail sales and management. They also see how diligently people work in preparing for jobs. They listen to the director as he explains that the Opportunities Industrialization Center offers training to unemployed, underemployed, and disadvantaged so that all people will become better citizens and enjoy a better life. Appraisal of outcomes of the study trips show that pupils gain information about job training and confidence in being able to get a job when they are adults.

When the schools make their annual report to the Board of Trustees, they point out the advances made on fundamental curriculum matters. The achievement of girls and boys in reading, mastering arithmetic, and furthering their knowledge of each subject is reported along with observations of their development in such activities as orchestra, glee club, and seasonal sports. Through the efforts of Mr. X, the annual report to the School Board now includes evidence of the girls' and boys' increased readiness for employment. When the annual report is published in the local newspaper, it is read by parents and other interested people of the community, and increases their confidence in what the schools are doing to help girls prepare for employment as well as family responsibilities.

The preceding statement illustrates many points brought out regarding the development of school innovations with the consent and aid of parents, especially the following:

1. The school should use newspapers and other communication media to make clear its point of view regarding matters of concern to parents.

2. Plans for innovation should grow out of assessment of pupil needs.

3. Spread of ideas among school personnel should precede and parallel spread of ideas through the community.

4. The acceptance of an idea or plan for program improvement should not be left to chance nor taken for granted.

5. Developmental work on a new program, or on program involvement, requires more time and attention than does the continued cultivation of the program once it has been incorporated into the curriculum.

6. Continuing evaluation and appraisal of the effectiveness of program improvements are an essential part of innovations.

7. School and parent leaders should work together in taking responsibility for improvement of school programs.

Chapter Ten

PREPARING SCHOOL
PERSONNEL
FOR PARENT
CONFERENCES

The ultimate decision to organize parent-teacher conferences on a systemwide basis rests with the school administration. Prior to making that decision and with the approval of the administration, however, individual elementary schools initiate pilot projects based on the strong conviction of the principal and the teaching staff that the school's goals for children can be realized only as parents and teachers have opportunity for direct contact resulting in cooperative effort. Because of such successful pilot projects the request may come from principals, teachers, individual parents, parent-teacher associations or other community groups to extend the program of parent conferences to all schools in the system.

Initiating a Program of Parent-Teacher Conferences

The experienced administrator usually proceeds to test the strength of the request by asking the pilot school staff to prepare a report on its experience with parent-teacher conferences and make recommendations on the proposal to extend the procedure throughout the school system. The administrator may suggest that the report and recommendations become the subject for study and consideration at parent-teacher association meetings, staff meetings at individual schools, principals' meetings and at meetings of other professional organizations interested in the subject. Meanwhile the librarian develops a collection of books, bulletins, pamphlets and magazine articles on parent-teacher conferences and the availability of these resources is publicized through the usual avenues of communication. Resources of nearby colleges and universities are examined and persons identified who can give leadership in the exploration of the subject. As a result, an extension course may be organized for teachers who wish to study the subject thoroughly; professional organizations in the system may cooperate by engaging well qualified persons to talk on the subject at their regular meetings; and other nearby school systems where conferences have been initiated may be invited to share their experience.

After sufficient time has elapsed so that all the teachers and many of the parents are aware of the proposal under consideration, a meeting may be held at which a panel representative of persons who have been involved in the exploratory activities presents the topic from the point of view of the parents, the teachers, the school principals, the district parent-teacher association council, and other individuals and groups. Since the children have probably been aware of the proposal under consideration, the reaction of the children may be sought by teachers in classroom discussions. A representative child or two may also participate in the panel.

If the consensus of opinion appears to be in favor of a systemwide plan of parent-teacher conferences, decision by the properly constituted administrative authority comes as a matter of course.

The question may be raised concerning why such time-consuming procedures are used. If the administration is convinced that parent-teacher conferences are sound and likely to prove beneficial to children, why not decide immediately to institute the program and notify the staff concerning the date the decision becomes effective?

Obviously, extensive study and consultation prior to decision means that many persons are involved. They participate in determining values and in anticipating the problems which must be resolved in implementing the program. Problems of how many conferences to hold annually, length of time necessary for each conference, scheduling, using the conference as the method of reporting pupil progress to parents versus traditional report cards, pupil participation in conferences, and many other problems will have been considered as a result of the challenge inherent in the proposal. Solutions which seem to meet the needs of everyone may emerge and obstacles which at first seemed insuperable may disappear.

General support of the procedure is thus assured before a final policy decision is reached.

A planned period for deliberation helps teachers and parents adjust to the new idea and prevents the shock of an official announcement which requires an adjustment on the part of both parent and teacher to a new and potentially threatening relationship. Many worthwhile innovations in education generate community resistance and must be discarded because sufficient time and study have not been given to guarantee general support. The preliminary planning period affords contact with school personnel. Group meetings of the parents of the children in each classroom provide an initial opportunity for meeting the teacher and discussing an educational problem in a small, intimate and friendly group. Initial fears are lessened as parents talk together about the purpose of conferences, how they will be conducted, and the responsibilities of the parents. In some situations it may be possible to show a motion picture of a parent-teacher conference[1] so parents may observe other persons in the role that they will assume in the proposed relationship.

Preparation of Teachers for Working with Parents

In the professional preparation of many teachers little time was given in the past to training them in conducting conferences. Teachers were understandably reluctant to engage in an activity in which they felt inadequately prepared. But with carefully planned in-service preparation and some experience in conducting conferences, teachers soon feel more secure. Many teachers express appreciation of the fact that they find their work with children more satisfactory following conferences with their parents. Support of the home is quickly reflected in more productive effort and better attitudes.

Administrators follow a variety of ways to provide in-service preparation. An extension course from a college or university has been previously mentioned as one systematic way of preparing teachers for successful conferences. Such courses may be pursued in summer session or during the school year. More informal in-service workshops and discussion groups with thoroughly competent leadership are sometimes preferred because they make it possible to adjust the training more specifically to the needs of the particular community.

[1] *Open For Discussion*, A Series of Parent-Teacher Conferences. For information address: Special Purpose Films, 26740 Latigo Shore Drive, Malibu, California.

Whatever method is used, experience has shown that certain activities provide fruitful ways to enhance the teacher's professional skills. The training program should begin by helping teachers to feel that regularly scheduled parent-teacher conferences will make their relations with the children more effective and that with experience they can become as efficient in working with adults as with children.

Among the techniques successfully used in training sessions are the following:

1. Discussion following study of scripts that report parent-teacher conferences
2. Role playing of parent-teacher conferences
3. Examination of anecdotal records for material of interest to parents
4. Compilation of a sample folder for each child's work
5. Development of helpful forms to use as a basis for a conference
6. Answering questions the parents often ask
7. Listing praiseworthy behavior to observe in pupils and report to their parents.

Study of reports of conferences. It is almost impossible to observe an actual parent-teacher conference without causing self-consciousness on the part of the participants. This is apt to distort their relationship. As a substitute for observation, scripts of conferences which have been written to illustrate a specific point, or scripts of actual conferences that have been recorded on tapes and transcribed, are frequently used in in-service training. Each report is followed by questions for discussion.

REPORT ON CONFERENCE

Parent: Hello, you are Christine's teacher, Mrs. Carpenter, aren't you?

Teacher: Yes, indeed. Come right on in. I'm so happy to see you again. We didn't have much time to talk the first day of school when you brought Christine to kindergarten.

Parent: No, I was almost late for work. But I took time off today for two conferences with teachers. You know my son Ronald is in the second grade and I am really worried about him because he is having so much trouble with reading.

Teacher: Miss Greene is an excellent teacher. She has had special training in the teaching of reading. I am confident about a solution to Ronald's problem. I know Ronald. He calls for Christine and is her wonderful big brother whom she is always talking about.

Parent: Yes, they get along well and Ronald is a responsible little fellow. But, of course, you want to talk about Christine.

Teacher: Of course, I do. I enjoy having Christine in kindergarten. She is full of ideas and enters into all the activities with the greatest enthusiasm. She is a friendly child and is well liked by the other children.

Parent: I'm glad to know that she is getting along well. Perhaps you could tell me something I can do so she won't have trouble with reading later on. You don't start them in reading in kindergarten, do you?

Teacher: No, we don't start reading in kindergarten. We believe most five-year-olds benefit by a program of rich experiences in science, stories and poems, music, art, rhythmical activities, block play and by developing a large vocabulary of words they can use in speaking. We put great emphasis in kindergarten on oral language development as the best preparation for later success in reading.

Parent: Well, I just thought if Chris started reading early we might avoid Ron's trouble.

Teacher: I understand how you feel, but truly Chris will make better progress if we don't rush her into learning experiences for which she is not ready. One thing to remember when people talk about teaching reading to the very young is that five-year-olds are normally far-sighted. So, I am sure young eyes should avoid tasks that require too much near vision.

Parent: I know you are right, but isn't there *anything* I can do to help?

Teacher: Indeed, there is. By all means read to your children at home. Children who have been read to a lot, who have listened to interesting stories, look forward to being able to read for themselves. Chris always sits as near to me as she can when I begin to read or tell a story.

Parent: Maybe I won't be as good at it as you are, Mrs. Carpenter, but I'll try. Chris loves kindergarten. She never has time enough to tell me about all the exciting things that happen. I want her to have a good time in school, not such a hard time as Ronnie is having.

Teacher: You can stop at the Public Library on your way home. The Children's Librarian, Mrs. Langer, will be happy to suggest books suitable to read to the children and you can borrow them on your library card.

Parent: That's a good idea. I'll do it. Thank you for talking with me about Ronnie. I know Chris is going to get along all right. She is smart like her Daddy. Ron's more like me.

Teacher: Then he is an especially nice person, I think. Please let me know how the reading at home works out.

Suggested Questions

1. *How did the teacher handle the problem which was deeply concerning the parent?*
2. *Should the teacher have insisted on discussing Christine's adjustment to school?*
3. *Did the parent leave the conference with positive help and reassurance?*
4. *What does Christine probably tell her parents about school? Did the parent give any clues?*
5. *How do you think Miss Greene developed her conference with Ronald's mother? Use role playing to present your plan for the conference.*

REPORT OF CONFERENCE

Teacher: Good afternoon, Mrs. Wright. I am so glad you felt well enough to come for this conference. Marvin told me you have been quite ill. He is getting back to normal since you came home from the hospital.

Parent: I really looked forward to talking with you today. I know these past weeks have been hard on Marvin and I wanted to know how he is getting along in his school work.

Teacher: We adults are so likely to expect children to do their school work with the same energy no matter what is happening to them in their out-of-school lives. We don't do so well ourselves when we are worried and unhappy. Marvin has shown me how the bottom drops out of the world of an eight-year-old when his mother is seriously ill.

Parent: Marvin told me you asked every day about how I was getting along and talked with him often about what he was doing after school.

Teacher: With you home again, I expect Marvin's smile to be restored completely. He will soon be working in his usual efficient way. But your illness has made me recognize what an exceedingly sensitive little boy we are dealing with.

Parent: I was surprised that he was so distressed. I really thought he took me pretty much for granted.

Teacher: You know, I keep a file for each child with a selection of his paintings during the year. Let me spread them out so we can take a look at them. These were Marvin's paintings before your illness began.

Parent: How gay and colorful—and amusing too.

Teacher: This is the picture he painted the day you went to the hospital. Nothing gay and colorful there! The interesting thing about these paintings is that Marvin wanted to paint every day. Painting seemed to afford him a way to express feelings that he couldn't put into words.

The pictures surely seem to show that Marvin has had a traumatic experience, but they also indicate that he finds relief and solace in artistic expression.

Parent: I must be a bit like Marvin, Miss Marcotti. I find it difficult to put what I am feeling into words, but I will think about what you have said for a long time.

Suggested Questions

1. How did the teacher show her concern for people with problems?

2. How did the teacher's observation of the child's behavior deepen her insight?

3. Was this an appropriate or an inappropriate subject to discuss at a parent-teacher conference?

4. *What do you think was the parent's attitude toward the school and teacher as a result of this conference?*

5. *What might occur when Miss Marcotti sees Marvin's mother a month later at a Parent-Teacher Association meeting? Use role playing to show the incident.*

REPORT OF CONFERENCE

Parent: I'm Mrs. Gibbs, Tommy's mother.

Teacher: I am happy to meet you, Mrs. Gibbs. Tommy is a new boy in our school this year and I am glad to have an opportunity to talk with you about his school work.

Parent: Things are so different here from his previous school that I have lots of questions I want to ask.

Teacher: Good, that's why we have conferences. You have already told me that Tommy has been talking about what we are doing. Does he like school?

Parent: Yes, he seems to like school here. But we want to be sure he is learning something, not just having a good time.

Teacher: I believe we learn best when we are happy, Mrs. Gibbs. I am glad Tommy is enjoying school because we are enjoying him.

Parent: Well, we know that learning to read is the most important thing children learn in school. But Tommy says he doesn't read aloud every day. He says you have something called "individualized reading." My neighbor says that is just helping children select library books. She said that one child doesn't read a paragraph after another child. How can they learn to read if they don't have a turn reading?

Teacher: You really have been thinking about this reading problem, haven't you, Mrs. Gibbs? Let's see if I can explain. First, Tommy is a capable reader for his age and grade. I have heard him read orally a number of times not only from readers and library books but from science and social studies material as well.

Parent: Well, I am relieved to hear that he reads pretty well. I keep after him to study at home and improve his reading.

Teacher: I have checked Tommy carefully on his word perception, on his grasp of meaning, on his reaction to what he has read, and on how well he relates the ideas obtained from his reading to his previous experience. In my judgment he is a good reader, but he needs to broaden his reading interests, and there is where you can help Tommy most.

Parent: Is this "individualized reading?"

Teacher: In a way, but we want to talk about other things as well as reading. I have here an article by one of our leading educators: "What is Individualized Reading?" Would you like to take it along and read it? It is my only copy and I shall appreciate your returning it by Tommy when you are finished with it.

Parent: Thank you. It is kind of you to lend me your copy. I'll let my neighbor read it, too, if that is all right with you.

Teacher: By all means. Now, about Tommy. He needs praise and encouragement to do his best. I have learned that in the short time he has been with me. He positively glows when I praise him for a job well done.

Parent: We aren't much for praise. It's so easy to spoil children.

Teacher: And the other thing to discover is how we can work together to help Tommy broaden his reading interests.

Parent: We could buy him some books if you would suggest some.

Teacher: Good. We also have an excellent school library and a good public library. Once Tommy's interests are aroused, he will go to books naturally to extend his information.

Parent: Well, I can't for the life of me think what else we can do. What do you suggest?

Teacher: Since you and your family are newcomers to this community, maybe you would like to take trips to places of interest near here. Some trips you can make by bus; for some, you will need to use your car. Here is a list of the cultural resources of this community. A committee of teachers developed it last year. It tells where to go, how to get there, and what to see.

Parent: And you think that going to these parks, museums, planetariums, art galleries, and other places I see here in this book will broaden Tommy's reading interests?

Teacher: I'm sure of it.

Parent: Well, we surely will try it then. Some of these places sound really interesting. I'll enjoy seeing them myself.

Teacher: I am certain you will. Maybe Tommy can let me know where you go, and I can keep track of any new reading interests that seem related to these experiences.

Here is Mr. Roberts for my next conference. I have enjoyed planning with you. We will look forward to our results. Goodbye, Mrs. Gibbs.

Suggested Questions

1. *How did the parent respond to the explanation about the child's reading?*
2. *Did the teacher's explanation block or further communication?*
3. *What two positive principles did the teacher attempt to establish?*
4. *Was rapport improved and greater confidence developed?*
5. *What is the possibility that this parent will learn some more effective child rearing practices than those she now uses?*
6. *If Mrs. Gibbs personally returns the article, "What Is Individualized Reading?" she can talk further with Tommy's teacher. With another teacher, use role playing to dramatize this conference.*

Role playing. Role playing provides an excellent way for a group of teachers to grow in conference skill. With written descriptions of the conference situation provided, a member of the group accepts the role of the parent, another the role of the teacher. Then a parent-teacher conference is held using the data supplied. Observers in the group can then analyze the strengths and weaknesses of the conference. Roles can then be reversed so that the player identifies with the other person. Sometimes others in the group will take the two roles to show another way in which the parent-teacher conference could proceed. Here is an example of a written description to serve as a springboard for role playing.

Miss Escobar has been concerned about Peter's frequent tardiness. Although she is not a rigid person with inflexible rules, she finds that Peter's arrival fifteen or twenty minutes late is disruptive. Peter needs much individual help with his work, and it is difficult for him to keep his attention on the task in hand. Peter is eight years old, in the second grade, and the oldest child in a family of four. He is well cared for and gets along reasonably well with the other children. Miss Escobar plans to discuss the tardiness particularly when Mrs. Wilson comes for her first conference of the school year.

The teachers in a workshop in which role playing had been profitably used each agreed to write a brief description of a situation which incorporated one of the most difficult problems with which she had to cope. They protected persons by using fictitious names. These situations were used for role playing and nearly everyone agreed that they resulted in many useful suggestions regarding ways to meet the specific problem.

The teachers in the same workshop thought it useful to develop a set of criteria to use in evaluating a parent-teacher conference. They agreed that the following were characteristics of a good conference and could be used by a teacher to evaluate a conference. Since the teacher sets the tone and guides the discussion, the criteria were in terms of the teacher's behavior:

CRITERIA FOR EVALUATING A CONFERENCE

1. The teacher was friendly.
2. The teacher made the parent feel comfortable.
3. The teacher let the parent express her concerns.
4. The teacher listened to the parent understandingly and appreciatively.
5. The teacher made no attempt to tell the parent how to manage her family.
6. The teacher focused attention on the child.
7. The teacher emphasized a particular strength of the child on which parent and teacher could build.
8. The teacher described a remediable weakness on which they could work.
9. The teacher suggested ways by which she and the parents could work together.
10. The teacher encouraged the parent in feeling that the school appreciates her child and feels that she has an important role to play in her child's education.

Use of anecdotal records. Many teachers become quite proficient in recording day-by-day incidents about individual children. These are kept in the child's cumulative file. Prior to a parent-teacher conference, teachers review these records. The records are always dated so they can be arranged in sequence for further study. One teacher's record of the behavior of an unusually aggressive boy changed long established parental behavior in which ridicule, shouting and physical punishment were used in disciplining the child. An exceedingly hostile father was convinced that his advice to his son, "If anyone hits you, you hit him back and hard," was most reprehensible. But he learned it only after the aggressive child had destroyed the vision in the eye of a child who had accidentally pushed him.

Nothing is more effective in a parent-teacher conference than the brief descriptions of episodes in the life of a child. If a teacher is attempting to build patterns of cooperation, each description of increasingly cooperative behavior is cause for satisfaction. Each uncooperative act calls for a reexamination of the teacher's ways of guiding the child.

Compilation of individual folders. Many schools encourage their teachers in compiling a simple folder for each child. This compilation is a good teaching and conference technique because it tells the child and his parents that work he has done is valuable enough to keep for further use. If a few papers, pictures, and compositions are kept each week, dated and arranged seriatim, they tell the story of a child's progress better than innumerable words. A sudden deterioration in quality will send parents and teacher on a serious search for causes.

Development of useful forms. In schools that appreciate the importance of parent conferences, the question arises: "Shall we develop a form for use in parent conferences?" Many teachers prefer to use no forms during a conference and record immediately after the conference any information they consider pertinent. Others find it is helpful to use a form which has identification data—name of child, school, teacher and date and space for notes on three sets of entries:

> Strengths observed by parent
> Strengths observed by teacher
>
> Needs observed by parent
> Needs observed by teacher
>
> Suggestions for home
> Suggestions for school

The use of such a form may be helpful in planning for each conference so that strengths as well as needs are considered. Parents are usually impressed by the planning the teacher has done, the kind of information about the child she has brought together to share, and the thoughtful suggestions about how a situation may be helped at home and at school.

Some schools use a form for conference notes with a carbon so that parents may have a copy of the items discussed and the action upon which agreement has been reached.

Answering parents' questions. In preparing for parent conferences, individual teachers and groups of teachers find it helpful to think about children as their families do. Schools are often a subject of discussion in family and social groups. Many families plan their lives around the daily and annual schedule of the school. Meals are served so children can catch the bus or otherwise get to school on time. Outings are planned for weekends, and vacations for school holidays. These facts bear testimony to the profound concern parents have in safeguarding the educational opportunity of their child.

To be sure, there is the occasional family that takes children out of school for trips during the school year. There are families that expect, and even demand, welfare services from the school. And still others who relinquish as much responsibility for their children to the school as possible. These are the families that constitute a source of worry and irritation. Because of the concern teachers feel, they are apt to lose perspective and think that there are more such families than there actually are.

But regardless of whether parents approach their obligations to their children with responsibility or irresponsibility, all have many questions they would like to have answered. Some schools use various means of securing information about questions parents ask and attempt to provide information through mass media of communication.

Education is exceedingly complex and teachers frequently have difficulty in giving a satisfactory answer to a parent's question. A book by Dr. Nancy Larrick, *A Parent's Guide to Children's Education,* should be accessible in every elementary school.[2] When a parent raises a question, the teacher may say: "I will be glad to answer your question, but first let's look to see if Dr. Larrick has an answer to your question. Then we can discuss it further. Many educators throughout the country read this

---

[2] Nancy Larrick, *A Parent's Guide to Children's Education.* New York: Trident Press, 1963.

manuscript before the book was published and offered suggestions, so the answers represent more than one person's judgment." Parents are favorably impressed to find that *their* question has already been considered sufficiently important to have been studied and answered by a reputable educator in a book published by a reputable publisher.

Listing praiseworthy pupil behavior. In preparing school personnel for parent conferences, it is worthwhile to review what is expected of pupils. A group of teachers discusses the school objectives, and thinks about how to state these colloquially to facilitate communicating with parents. "We think it is important for children to be proud of their school and keep it neat and clean," is more meaningful to most parents than is a statement such as, "Maintenance of school property is a school objective."

The individual teacher is encouraged to think about how to state simply the curriculum objectives for her grade level. "We want the children to be able to buy something at the store and get the correct change," is more meaningful to a parent than saying, "We are teaching the children the process of subtraction." Furthermore, the parents can reinforce what the school is doing by providing out-of-school opportunities for making a small purchase.

In the process of reviewing teaching objectives for use in parent conferences, the teachers usually further their own understanding of the objectives and of the importance of working with parents. Such understanding on the part of teachers is of direct benefit to children.

The Content of the Conference

The techniques presented in this chapter have been some of the ones considered most helpful in handling parent conferences. Far more important, to be sure, is the fact that the conference affords opportunity for a teacher to share knowledge obtained through professional training with persons who can use it as parents.

The profession must give further attention to what information can be shared in this way. Teachers have studied human growth and development. Parents need this knowledge. Teachers have studied about the relation of child rearing practices in homes and educational problems in schools. Parents need this knowledge too. Teachers are constantly working on curriculum—the experiences the school provides to foster development. Parents, also, need to know about the curriculum. Parent-teacher conferences need not be trivial and inconsequential. They can satisfy a need for more knowledge on the part of people who are making important decisions concerning young human beings.

One of the most important responsibilities of the professor who prepares a student to teach, and of the school administrator who furthers her development, is to encourage her in communicating effectively not only with children but also with their parents.

On-the-Job Improvement of Parent-Teacher Relationships

A continuing responsibility of administrative personnel in the schools is to help teachers improve their ability to work with parents for the good of children. This responsibility is carried out by arranging opportunities for teachers to learn what they should do in working with parents. But before such learning is complete the teachers must also know what not to do. A teacher learns this in service when her school provides suitable guidance for interaction with parents.

Planning for Further Parent Participation

The major focus in this book has been on effective communication between parents and teachers regarding the individual child's growth and development and his progress in the educational program provided by society to facilitate the achievement of his potential. This relationship between parents and teachers is the most important of all community relationships. The school cannot achieve its objectives for children unless such a relationship can be developed and maintained throughout the child's entire period of elementary schooling. School systems are challenged to discover and initiate effective ways to provide opportunity for mothers, fathers, and teachers to be in the closest possible communication about their mutual responsibility for rearing and educating children. When a well designed system of parent-teacher conferences has been successfully incorporated as an integral part of the educational system, new vistas of cooperative involvement and participation of parents appear. Learning to work together on important and at the same time emotionally charged problems paves the way for a variety of endeavors to improve the educational opportunity of all children.

In the years ahead, parents and other community members will play a greater role in curriculum making. Such participation is not new.

Forward-looking school systems have long recognized that the complexity of school problems requires active community help and support.

Demands are constantly being made upon the school to provide an enriched curriculum, to provide special education programs adapted to the wide variety of children with special learning problems, and to provide new health and guidance services. These demands for quality education are as strongly supported by school people as they are by interested lay citizens. They cannot be met, however, without consideration of problems of finance, school facilities, and teacher supply.

Parents and teachers alike need to understand that schools are not the only educative agency operating in the community. The home, the neighborhood, the playground, the church, recreation programs, children's organizations, and welfare services are all agencies for the education of the young. These groups need a common meeting ground for discussion of their purposes, the relation of the purposes of each to the others, the educative process, how each group can help to implement and appraise the school program, and how all the programs can be coordinated to secure the greatest output in terms of human effort and financial resources.

The school which works with parents of all the children of the community is probably in the most strategic position to provide the meeting ground for a coordinating system. Domination by any group or agency would prove destructive in such a democratic enterprise; all must feel a common responsibility in the community's care of its children.

Parents and other citizens provide valuable resources in instruction. The explosion of knowledge makes it impossible for any teacher to know enough about new developments to satisfy children who are interested in space exploration, satellites, oceanography, city planning, rapid transportation systems, or a score of other subjects intriguing to children. But nearly every community has members with experiences, skills, interests, and materials which they will willingly share with a group of children. Certain school systems keep a file of resource people available. A note or a telephone call will usually result in planning a convenient time for the adult to meet with an interested class.

Innumerable other ways that parents can work with schools will occur to school people who recognize the long-range values of parent involvement. Parents are frequently willing to participate in a study trip to a museum, an art gallery, an airport, an industrial plant, or a center of historical interest. Parents are willing to volunteer valuable time to assist in the maintenance of the elementary school library or instructional materials center. Parents sometimes assist in kindergarten and primary grades so that children have more opportunity to work individually with a sympathetic adult. Special skills which children wish to learn such as sewing, knitting and embroidery are available through willing community members. Skillful persons in many of the industrial arts, in construction and in sports take genuine pleasure in sharing their knowledge and skill with children. World travelers, equipped with slides and their specially selected treasures, can make the places they have visited vivid to children.

Compared with other service agencies such as hospitals and social welfare organizations, schools have made relatively little use of the reservoir of volunteer service available in nearly every community. Important as these and countless other contributions are to enliven the day-by-day operation of schools, the greatest value to the school is in the moral support people give who really understand the problems that confront the school.

Children appreciate their school more when important adults in the community take time to come to the school. Such adult participants are excellent interpreters of the services of the school because they have a sense of truly belonging to the organization.

In these days of change and innovation on every intellectual frontier, far too few of the many educational "projects" being developed give attention to the home-school-community relationship. But no area is more challenging to creative social planning and no area is more promising. Education may have within its grasp the machinery essential not only to bring about basic improvement in educational service but also to accomplish the fundamental democratic task of human conservation.

SELECTED BOOKS, BULLETINS, AND PAMPHLETS

Bailard, Virginia and Strang, Ruth, *Parent-Teacher Conferences.* New York: McGraw-Hill Book Company, Inc., 1964.

Bettelheim, Bruno, *Dialogs with Mothers.* New York: The Macmillan Company, 1962.

Department of Classroom Teachers, National Education Association; National Congress of Parents and Teachers; National School Public Relations Association, *The First Big Step.* Washington, D.C.: National School Public Relations Association, 1966.

Doll, Ronald C. and Fleming, Robert S., Editors, *Children Under Pressure.* Columbus, Ohio: Charles E. Merrill Books, Inc., 1966.

Department of Elementary-Kindergarten-Nursery Education, *Prevention of Failure.* Washington, D.C.: National Education Association, 1965.

D'Evelyn, Katherine, *Individual Parent-Teacher Conferences.* New York: Bureau of Publications, Teachers College, Columbia University, 1963.

Fusco, Gene C., *School-Home Partnership in Depressed Urban Neighborhoods.* Washington, D.C.: U.S. Office of Education, 1964.

Gabbert, Hazel F., *Working with Parents,* Bulletin 1918 No. 7 (reprint). Washington, D.C.: U.S. Office of Education, 1960.

Hymes, James L., *Effective Home-School Relations.* Englewood Cliffs, New Jersey: Prentice-Hall, Inc., 1953.

Langdon, Grace and Stout, Irving W., *Helping Parents Understand Their Child's School.* Englewood Cliffs, New Jersey: Prentice-Hall, Inc., 1957.

Langdon, Grace and Stout, Irving W., *Teacher-Parent Interviews.* Englewood Cliffs, New Jersey: Prentice-Hall, Inc., 1954.

Leonard, Edith M., Van Deman, Dorothy D., and Miles, Lillian E., *Counseling with Parents in Early Childhood Education.* New York: The Macmillan Company, 1954.

National School Public Relations Association and Association of Classroom Teachers, *Conference Time for Parents and Teachers.* Washington, D.C.: National Education Association, 1961.

Osborne, Ernest Glenn, *The Parent-Teacher Partnership.* New York: Bureau of Publications, Teachers College, Columbia University, 1959.

Redl, Fritz, *When We Deal with Children.* New York: The Free Press, 1967.

Reeves, Charles E., *Parents and the School: A Guide to Cooperation in Child Development.* Washington, D.C.: Public Affairs Press, 1963.

Ruben, Margarete; Dancoff, Martha, et al., *Parent Guidance in the Nursery School.* New York: International Universities Press, 1960.

Stout, Irving W. and Langdon, Grace, "Parent-Teacher Relationships," # 16 in *What Research Says to the Teacher.* Washington, D.C.: National Education Association, Department of Classroom Teachers, 1958.

INDEX